The African Texans

TEXANS ALL

A Series from
the Institute of Texan Cultures
Sara R. Massey, General Editor

The African Texans

jaxon·02

Alwyn Barr

TEXAS A&M UNIVERSITY PRESS · COLLEGE STATION

The Ellwood Foundation, Houston, Texas, provided funding
support for the research and writing of this book.

The paper used in this book meets the minimum requirements
of the American National Standard for Permanence
of Paper for Printed Library Materials, Z39.48-1984.
Binding materials have been chosen for durability.
∞

Illustrations on title page and chapter heads are
details from map by Jack Jackson found on page 2.

Library of Congress Cataloging-in-Publication Data

Barr, Alwyn.
    The African Texans / Alwyn Barr.—1st ed.
        p. cm.—(Texans all)
    Includes bibliographical references and index.
    ISBN 1-58544-321-2 (alk. paper)—
    ISBN 1-58544-350-6 (pbk.: alk. paper)
    1. African Americans—Texas—History. 2. Free African Americans—
Texas—History. 3. Slaves—Texas—History. 4. Freedmen—Texas—History.
5. African Americans—Migrations—History. 6. Migration, Internal—United
States—History. 7. Texas—Social conditions. 8. Texas—Race relations.
I. University of Texas Institute of Texan Cultures at San Antonio.
II. Title.   III. Series.
E185.93.T4B36   2004
976.4'00496073—dc22   2003016357

Contents

Illustrations

Foreword

The Institute of Texan Cultures opened in 1968 with exhibits depicting the cultural groups that settled early Texas. The exhibit displays resulted from a massive research effort by many young scholars into the history and culture of Texas. This research served as the basis for writing what became known as "the ethnic pamphlet series." The series included pamphlets devoted to such titles as the Swiss Texans, the Norwegian Texans, the Native American Texans, the Mexican Texans, the Greek Texans, the Spanish Texans, the African American Texans, the Chinese Texans, and many more. Some years later several books about additional cultural groups were produced. These included the Japanese Texans, the Irish Texans, the Polish Texans, and numerous others.

Thirty years later, as staff reviewed the early pamphlets, it became obvious that although the material remained accurate, it was time for a revision with a fresh look. Thus emerged the Texans All book set. Organized by world regions, each volume briefly summarizes aspects of the social and cultural contributions made by the groups immigrating to Texas. The book series includes the five distinctive cultural groups that were in Texas or came to Texas before statehood and into the early twentieth century: *The Indian Texans, The Mexican Texans, The European Texans, The African Texans,* and *The Asian Texans.*

Each author used an organizational pattern dictated by the content. (*The African Texans* is organized chronologically, for instance.) The content of each book does not follow a traditional history of battles and events in Texas, but rather addresses the cultures and the people as they formed early communities in Texas. The authors utilized primary sources to incorporate into the text, and sidebars provide biographical or topical sketches. As the manuscripts neared completion, maps were commissioned to illustrate the settlement areas of the various cultural groups in Texas.

As the various immigrant groups adapted to the land and culture of others, and new generations were born and intermarried with other groups, their unique cultural identities began to weaken. For many their "old world" identity faded, and the ethnic origins of many communities began to disappear. With the twentieth-century exodus from rural communities to larger towns and cities, the distinctive cultural traditions and customs of rural communities further blurred.

Many of the people presented here are unknown because several of the stories are about ordinary people who struggled to build a home and make a living in Texas. The majority of the more than three hundred photographs used in the series are from the Institute of Texan Cultures Research Library's extensive photograph collection of over three million images relating to the people of Texas.

This story of Africans in Texas is not the same as other immigrants. While some came as free men and women, most were uprooted from their homelands in Africa and brought to Texas by force. Others came as property of the descendants of European immigrants who had settled in the United States.

Many books recount the struggle of African Americans against their oppressors and offer comprehensive historical overviews. The content here summarizes and provides examples of the social and cultural contributions made by African Texans as they built churches, formed schools, challenged the legal system, and sought economic opportunities to abolish the legacies of slavery and to stand proudly among the many diverse peoples of Texas.

Sara R. Massey

The African Texans

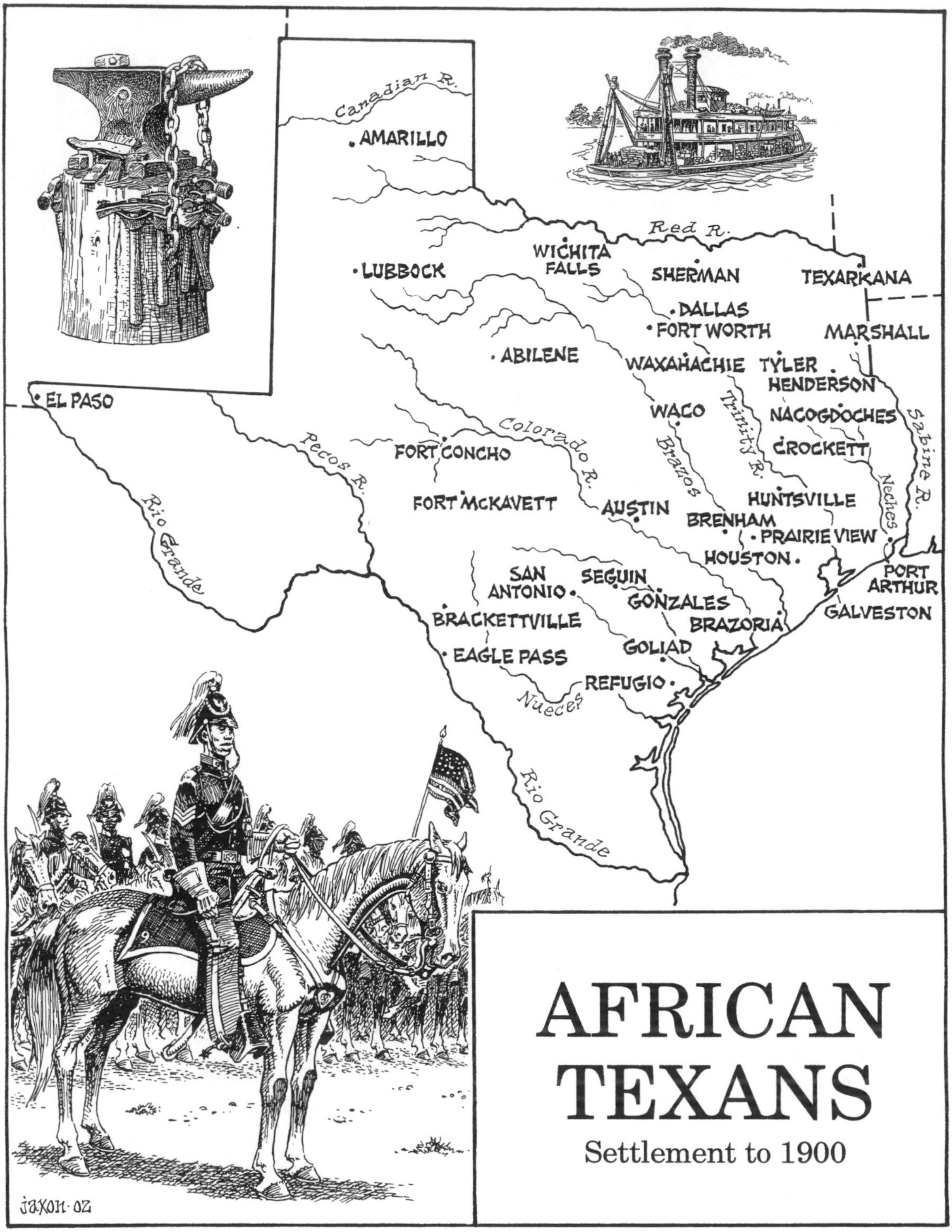
Canadian R.
AMARILLO
Red R.
LUBBOCK
WICHITA FALLS
SHERMAN
TEXARKANA
DALLAS
FORT WORTH
MARSHALL
ABILENE
WAXAHACHIE
TYLER
HENDERSON
EL PASO
WACO
Trinity R.
NACOGDOCHES
Sabine R.
Colorado R.
Brazos
CROCKETT
Pecos R.
FORT CONCHO
Neches
Rio Grande
FORT MCKAVETT
AUSTIN
HUNTSVILLE
BRENHAM
PRAIRIE VIEW
HOUSTON
SAN ANTONIO
SEGUIN
GONZALES
PORT ARTHUR
GALVESTON
BRACKETTVILLE
BRAZORIA
EAGLE PASS
GOLIAD
REFUGIO
Nueces
Rio Grande
jaxon·02
AFRICAN TEXANS
Settlement to 1900

African Texan settlement up to 1900. Map by Jack Jackson

Introduction

𝓕ROM THE SIXTEENTH CENTURY through the twenti-
eth century the lives of African people in Texas changed dramati-
cally. Within this span of four centuries, black Texans contributed
to the development and diversity of Texas culture in numerous
ways. This book expands our understanding of African American
history in Texas by providing examples of the social and cultural
contributions made by them, which have not received much attention. The bibliographical essay at the end of this volume offers
a guide for readers who wish to know more details about specific
topics.

This book is organized into five parts. The first section describes
free Africans before the Civil War, beginning in the Spanish colonial period with explorers and continuing with settlers under Spain,
Mexico, the Republic of Texas, and the United States. The early free
black men and women came primarily to build a new and prosperous life.

The focus then shifts to the lives of enslaved Africans before the
Civil War, with greater attention given to the period of the republic
and the state in the early 1800s. Within the limits imposed by slavery, black people worked and used a variety of creative skills. They
kept some control over their lives through family ties and religion.
They preserved their African heritage through music and folklore
when they celebrated their few holidays from long days of labor.
Many resisted the controls of slavery, sought freedom, and celebrated
its arrival at the end of the Civil War.

Life after emancipation brought new hopes and struggles to gain economic opportunities and a chance to participate in government. While most African Texans worked on farms, others labored on ranches and service jobs in towns. In those places they tried to create stable families, establish their own churches and schools, participate in various sports, and use their music for both jobs and entertainment.

In the early twentieth century, the African Texans faced several forms of discrimination but struggled to overcome violence and segregation to participate more fully in all aspects of life in Texas. Blacks found new jobs loading ships, building railroads, working in oil fields, making steel, and constructing ships. They moved in growing numbers to cities, where they established businesses and became attorneys and doctors, as well as writers and photographers, professional musicians, and athletes.

In the later years of the twentieth century, African Americans formed and joined various civil rights groups that went to court to regain the right to vote and to desegregate schools and other public places across Texas. As a result of their efforts in the civil rights movement, and as laws and public opinion changed, black Texans began to join in the full range of activities available to citizens of the state and nation.

▼▼▼

CHAPTER 1

Free African Americans
before the Civil War

THE FIRST AFRICAN who came to Texas landed on the Gulf Coast as one of the few men that survived a Spanish exploring expedition in 1528. Estevan brought with him skills and cultural ideas from Africa and Spain. He could speak Arabic because he had grown up in North Africa where it was the common language, and he had been captured by Spaniards who made him a slave. From them he learned Spanish. He had been Muslim but accepted Catholic Christianity, perhaps to improve his status with the Spaniards.

As shipwreck victims in Texas, he and a few Spaniards helped each other survive the hardships of a new land and the months as captives of Indians. To gain favor with the native people, Estevan assisted the Spaniards in providing medical treatment to Indians who were ill. When he and three other survivors gained their freedom and searched for Spanish settlements in what became Mexico, he acted as the scout. With his language ability he seemed better able than the others to communicate with the new groups of native peoples they met in their travels.[1]

Estevan was the first African to bring new forms of culture to Texas. Other Africans followed him and added to the cultures of the region with folklore and, later, written stories. They contributed a variety of religious views. Black Texans sang and played music in the style of their homeland. As members of families they provided each other with support and care. They brought with them

Drawing of Estevan, the first African in the land of Texas. Institute of Texan Cultures illustration no. 73-1105

the skills to fashion homes and furniture that showed artistic beauty. In later generations, they became teachers and founded schools and universities. African Texans eventually entered new areas of entertainment such as sports. The social and cultural contributions of black Texans increased the longer they lived and worked in a region.

▼▼▼

Like Estevan, other African slaves entered New Spain, which became Mexico, and for years included Texas. Many of their children gained freedom and often married Spanish settlers or Indians. In Spanish colonies such as Mexico and Texas, the Spanish had the greatest wealth. They viewed themselves as the best people, with Indians and Africans below them in importance. Persons with a Spanish parent and an African parent found their status and acceptance fell somewhere between those two groups. An individual who acquired money and bought land might be able to improve his or her status and acceptance in society.

Some slaves and a larger number of free blacks came to Spanish Texas as soldiers and musicians in exploring expeditions of the 1500s and 1600s. Then in the 1700s they joined Spanish expeditions with settlers going north to help establish towns. Some, like Felipe Elua of San Antonio, used their skills to grow food crops such as sugar cane and vegetables, as well as cotton. Others worked as weavers to produce cloth from the cotton. Several, including Pedro Ramirez, helped herd cattle near San Antonio or received land for their own ranches, like Narciso la Baume in the Nacogdoches area. These African Tejanos usually spoke Spanish, worshiped as Catholics, and by the 1790s accounted for 15 percent of the non-Indian people in Spanish Texas.[1]

In the early 1800s, especially after the people of Mexico gained their independence from Spain in 1823, a limited number of free blacks from the United States entered Mexican Texas. They sought greater personal freedom and opportunities, often living at the edge of settlements.

White Americans in the eighteenth and nineteenth centuries viewed themselves as superior to other people, especially Indians and Africans, based on a strong sense of differences. White Americans and Texans emphasized the differences of darker skin color as well as the cultural variations such as dress, language, and religion. In British culture, "black" and "white" had taken on negative and positive meanings, which stimulated negative attitudes toward people of darker complexion. These views were coupled with the desire of a growing number of landowners for inexpensive laborers to work the fields. Even African Americans who had gained their freedom encountered whites who feared that free blacks living near slaves would influence the slaves to seek freedom. Thus, slaveholders won the passage of laws that limited the legal, social, and political rights of all black people in the southern United States.

The largest group of free African Americans in Texas farmed in the new region, while some raised cattle. The Ashworth family, who owned small ranches and hundreds or even thousands of animals in their herds on the coastal plains near the Sabine River, were very successful. Others contributed a variety of skills to their new communities, such as blacksmith Greenbury Logan in Brazoria County, Houston barber Nelson Kavanaugh, innkeeper and freighter William Goyens in Nacogdoches, and fisherman James Richardson of Velasco.

When the Texas Revolution exploded in the 1830s, free blacks chose sides primarily based on their cultural surroundings. Those who lived in Mexican towns, spoke Spanish, held Catholic views, and shared Hispanic culture usually favored the Mexican government. Those who had come from the United States, spoke English, considered themselves Protestants, and lived among the white settlers usually favored the revolt.

In the second skirmish of the revolution at Goliad in the fall of 1835, Samuel McCullough, a free black farmer, fell wounded. When the Texans captured San Antonio in December, Greenbury Logan took a bullet in his arm that left him disabled. Among the American volunteers who died at Goliad in the spring of 1836, Peter Allen had been a musician. Free black ranchers in East Texas sent money and supplies to the Texas troops. In April, "Dick," the drummer, helped provide the marching music for Sam Houston's army that won the battle at San Jacinto.

After Texas gained its independence, white Texans passed laws based on their racial views and desire to protect and expand slavery. The white landowners needed the slaves to work their land and tend their animals to become prosperous. These laws stopped other free

William Goyens served as Sam Houston's interpreter to negotiate a treaty with the Cherokee Indians. Painting by Edward Mills. Institute of Texan Cultures, illustration no. 68-1104

"Dick" the drummer at the 1836 battle of San Jacinto. Painting by Kermit Oliver. Institute of Texan Cultures illustration no. 68-1111

▼▼▼

blacks from moving into the new republic and made it difficult for a slaveholder to emancipate or free a slave. Free African Texans would not be able to vote, buy property, offer court testimony in cases that involved whites, or marry anyone who was white. The laws did allow those free blacks that had lived in Texas before the revolution to remain there. The laws limiting property do not seem to have been fully enforced, although some free African Texans faced conflicts that resulted from such discrimination.

Mariah Carr of Marshall, Texas, cards and spins cotton to make thread, c. 1880s. Institute of Texan Cultures illustration no. 72-60

Because of the limitations on free blacks in the Republic of Texas, their numbers grew slowly. The census of 1850 recorded an official high of 397 but probably missed some because of the difficulty of accurately recording census data in scattered rural populations. One historian estimated that up to 800 free Africans might have lived in Texas in the 1850s.

While a majority of these free blacks continued to raise crops or cattle, others lived in the small but growing towns. Henry Sigler used his skill as a barber to earn his living in Galveston, as did Henry Tucker in Houston. Cary McKinney cared for horses in Galveston. The masonry skills of Andrew Bell kept him employed constructing buildings in San Antonio.

Black women contributed additional skills to life in Texas towns. Mary Madison served as a much-appreciated nurse for residents in Galveston. In Jefferson County, Charity Bird became a successful baker, selling cakes. Fanny McFarland saved the money she earned as a laundress and bought land in Houston. Carolyn Logan assisted her husband who owned a tavern. A black woman in Eagle Pass managed a boarding house. Others earned a living sewing for neighbors in their communities.

Because of their small numbers free blacks lived scattered about with only a few in any county. Some free Africans married white husbands or wives. They lived among the Anglo or Mexican populations in communities where they probably did not develop their own churches or retain as much of a separate culture as did the much larger group of slaves in Texas. Although they generally could not send their children to schools taught by whites, parents instructed their own sons and daughters in reading and writing. Thus 60 to 70 percent of the free Africans in Texas had become literate by the 1850s. In addition, parents passed on the numerous practical skills they had learned.[3]

CHAPTER 2
Enslaved African Americans before the Civil War

SLAVERY DEVELOPED on a limited scale in Texas under Spain, and it appeared to be dying out by the nineteenth century. In the 1820s, after Mexico gained independence, the Mexican government abolished slavery but allowed settlers from the United States to bring slaves into Texas as indentured servants. Thus, slavery continued under another name. White Americans, primarily from the South, used slaves mainly as agricultural workers on farms and plantations growing cotton, sugar cane, and food crops such as corn. By the time of the Texas Revolution in 1835 the number of slaves had grown to about 5000. The new republic legalized slavery, as did the state government when Texas accepted annexation to the United States in 1846. Slaveholders and slave traders brought a growing number of African Americans to Texas between 1836 and 1860. Slaves numbered over 180,000—30 percent of the state's population. The growth rate of the slave population far surpassed the growth rate of the white population.

Some bondsmen had walked hundreds of miles to Texas, often connected by ropes that limited the possibility of escape. Slave women faced the dangerous moment of giving birth in a wagon along the trail, while others grieved the death of a child they had to leave in a roadside grave. Other enslaved people came to Texas on crowded ships, sometimes in chains, including slaves smuggled ashore from Africa, Cuba, and other West Indies islands. Slaveholders

The Weekly Telegraph *of Houston in 1859 ran advertisements selling slaves.* Institute of Texan Cultures illustration no. 100-465

moving to Texas often brought entire families of slaves, but other owners and traders sold family members separately. Jeff Hamilton found himself up for auction at the age of thirteen. "I stood on the slave block in the blazing sun for at least two hours . . . my legs ached. My hunger had become almost unbearable . . . I was filled with terror, and did not know what was to become of me. I had been crying for a long time."[1] Slave mothers pleaded or threatened suicide in an effort to keep their children.

Many slave women worked in the main house cooking in large, open hearths. Institute of Texan Cultures illustration no. 70-433

*The log cabin home of an
African American in Texas.*
Institute of Texan Cultures
illustration no. 75-1107

Slaves received no pay for their labor, beyond the basic necessities of food and clothing. They generally built their own cabins and raised and cooked their own food using what their owners did not want. Hog jowl, the small intestines of the hog (chitterlings), or pigs' feet supplemented with wild greens from the field served as the basis of many meals. Small game such as possum, squirrel, and rabbit as well as fish were added to the meals when available. Other readily available foods like cornmeal, sweet potatoes, sorghum, black-eyed peas, and beans rounded out their diet. Many of the black women worked as cooks in the homes of their owners. The cooking of these early black women has influenced the dietary habits of many Texans through the decades: ham hocks and black-eyed peas served with cornbread and sweet potato pie are still favorites.

▼▼▼

Jack Robison (1848–1925)

Jack Robison came to San Antonio with his master, who brought a herd of camels to Texas when the United States decided to experiment with raising camels. In San Antonio Jack was sold to W. A. Menger, owner of the Menger Hotel. Jack remembered rolling whiskey barrels to the storeroom while he worked at the Menger before he was sold again.

Joseph Ney of D'Hanis bought Jack on May 25, 1864, just a year before slaves were freed in Texas following the Civil War. Jack lived in the slaves' quarters and worked as a houseboy. His chores included milking the cow, hitching the horses to the carriage, feeding the chickens, and chopping wood for the fireplaces and kitchen stove.

In later years, after all the freed slaves left, Jack stayed on with the

Women and children also worked in the fields along side the men hoeing and picking cotton, which they then spun and wove into cloth for making clothes. Because slaveholders received the profits of slave labor and slaves received few other rewards as incentives, slaveholders needed elaborate controls to make their slaves work hard. Two types of controls existed: a series of laws adopted by the Republic of Texas and later by the state government, and punishments inflicted by individual slaveholders.

By law, slaves could not travel without a pass from their owners, possess weapons, gather in large groups, or have liquor without permission. Neither could they physically or verbally resist white control and supervision. Those who fought back, revolted, or tried to escape could be executed or whipped. Slaveholders had the authority to whip and punish slaves as they saw fit, although executing or maiming a slave could cause some legal problems as well as the lost value of the slave as property. They could chain slaves, sell them, and control their work time. Slaves could not legally marry, so a slave could be sold and, as a result, separated from family members entirely at the owner's discretion. Another common method of exerting control over slaves was to keep them uneducated. These actions, controls, and limitations, separately or together, forced cooperation from slaves, limited their ability to escape, and ensured their continued labor.

Work on farms and plantations included every slave from the age of about six. Small children gathered kindling for fires and helped feed chickens or pigs. Older boys and girls went to the fields with adult men and women to plough, plant seeds, hoe weeds, and pick cotton or harvest other crops. Male slaves cut cane on the sugar plantations near the coast or herded cattle on ranches in the same region. Slaves also cared for the horses and mules on farms. In the winter, they might cut down trees and brush to open new fields, or butcher cattle and hogs, or repair fences. Workdays generally began at first light and continued until dark, ten to twelve hours, except for holidays, Sundays, and a rare Saturday afternoon.

On larger farms and plantations some slave men became skilled

▼▼▼

Jack Robison, slave of Joe Ney, Sr., of D'Hanis, Texas, purchased May 25, 1864.
Institute of Texan Cultures illustration no. 102-85.1

Neys. Family members would move him from the old family homestead to stay and help out other family members, but he always returned to the Ney homestead, which he considered his home.

Jack died in 1925 and is buried in the segregated black Cottonwood Cemetery north of Hondo, Texas.

Source: Castro Colonies Heritage Association, Inc., *The History of Medina County, Texas* (Dallas: National Geographic Inc., n.d.), n. 525; tombstone, Cottonwood Cemetery, Hondo, Texas.

in specialized jobs such as blacksmithing and carpentry. Others might learn the crafts of brick laying, barrel making, repairing broken equipment, fashioning shoes, or tanning leather. Female slaves on large farms or plantations also became skilled as cooks, weavers, and seamstresses. The wealthiest planters might use a few slaves as personal servants and butlers or as gardeners and carriage drivers. In towns, most slave women worked in the homes of white families, while men labored loading ships and wagons, operating cotton presses, or freighting goods to warehouses. Others proved skilled in making saddles or as barbers and house builders.[2]

With this variety of skills, slaves created their own furniture and built their own one- or two-room log cabins. The slave craftsmen must have felt frustrated when they were directed to spend more time carefully constructing larger and nicer homes and furnishings for the slaveholders. Yet they were proud of their work.[3] Across Panola County a slave carpenter called Simpson worked with his owner constructing log homes for anyone willing to hire them.[4] Slave carpenters owned by the Ector family of Rusk County provided much of the skilled labor in the construction of a Presbyterian Church at Henderson.[5] In Central Texas, slave masons constructed an imposing house from limestone for their owner, Thomas Johnson.[6]

Once slave craftsmen had built houses, they often created the furnishings inside. Cary Davenport's father crafted his furniture as well as spinning wheels.[7] Furniture constructed by slave artisans ranged from chairs to desks and beds. Yach Stringfellow also described utensils and tools created by bondsmen around Brenham, such as handles for axes and hoes. To that list, Silvia King in Fayette County added carved spoons. In Washington County, slaves shaped wooden mortars for pounding grain and washtubs. Furthermore, mould board plows often came from the hands of slave craftsmen.[8]

Slave tanners produced a variety of other necessary items. Johnson Thompson remembered: "Pappy was the shoe-maker and he used wooden pegs of maple to fashion the shoes." Blacksmiths and other ironworkers created basic products for farming and use in houses. These included horseshoes, wheel rims, and metal plows, as well as andirons for the kitchens.[9]

Female slaves exhibited another set of skills. In Leon County, Mollie Watson explained, "All de women an' girls could spin an' weave an' nearly all of 'em could sew." Slave women made work clothes, but also material for the slaveholders. In Bosque County, a bondswoman received an award for the quality of her weaving.[10]

Other female slaves produced cloth from wool. In Gonzales County the women combined bark with parsley and copperas. A brown dye resulted, according to Ellen Polk. Or cloth could be dyed blue with indigo. Some slave women sewed cut up old clothes and cloth scraps into quilts with attractive patterns for use on beds in the winter. One pattern, remembered from the past, stitched to-

▼▼▼

Slave craftsmen made chairs from tree limbs such as the one shown in this 1890 photograph of a man living in Schulenburg, Texas. Institute of Texan Cultures illustration no. 80-249.1

Thornton Williams, a Masai, was captured in Africa and brought to America for sale. He was brought to Texas to work as a slave on the O'Connor Ranches. Institute of Texan Cultures illustration no. 96-1087

gether strips of cloth making what became known as string quilts.[11] Such quilts today are cherished remembrances of the past.

Women along with men made baskets from wood strips, according to Mary Edwards, who conveyed a sense of pride in the work. An African influence could be found in coiled baskets woven with pine needles and grass. Slaves also plaited (braided) bear grass into rope.[12]

In addition to practical crafts, slaves fabricated musical instruments out of a variety of materials. These included drums made from animal skins and wood, a flute from a buffalo horn, rattles from animal jaw bones, gourds shaped into fiddles or banjos, and whistles from tree bark.[13] Despite the limitations on their lives, Texas slaves used a wide range of skills that added to the folk art of the nineteenth century.

While slaves in Texas spent most of their lives working, they sustained themselves within the limits of the slave system through both individual and group actions. Family members provided a strong source of support for each other, despite a law that did not recognize slave marriages. Most slaveholders allowed slaves to choose a husband or wife from the plantation or a neighboring ranch. Thornton Wilder, who in 1862 rode with Dennis O'Connor to capture horses stolen by the Cherokee, provides an example of another type of marriage arrangement. Along with the horses, Thornton returned with a Cherokee woman whom he married. Some weddings among slaves involved simply hopping over a broom while others included a more elaborate celebration.

Owners encouraged slaves to have large families, which added to the number of workers they owned and thus increased their wealth. A few owners pressured slaves to have children without forming families, regardless of their feelings for each other. On plantations with larger numbers of bondsmen, both parents and children lived together unless sold. Probably a majority of slave children lived at least part of their lives in two-parent families. For those on smaller farms with only a few slaves, a husband and wife might live on neighboring farms and see each other during weekends and holidays. Peter and Judith Martin were such a couple. Peter and Judith came to

Sophia and Maria La Coste with their nursemaid Lidia in Brownsville, Texas, c. 1865. Institute of Texan Cultures illustration no. 85-433

Texas as slaves of Wylie Martin in Stephen F. Austin's Colony. Martin, who was frequently away on business, left Peter in charge of the farm. When Martin needed money, he sold Judith to the neighboring Jones family, where she raised their children, and Peter visited when possible. While growing up, slave children found themselves

▼▼▼

instructed on proper behavior and work chores by owners and on survival by their parents. In the words of historian Randolph Campbell: "Family ties gave slaves love, individual identity, and a sense of personal worth."[14]

The value slaves placed on family ties can be seen in the many cases when they ran away rather than be separated. Parents often gave their children the names of grandparents to affirm family connections. Some slaveholders kept families together if they had to sell slaves, but many owners did not. Other families faced separation through sales because of debts owed when the slaveholder died or as gifts of individual slaves to family members written into wills. Aaron Burleson gave Cecelia, a young slave girl, as a gift to his daughter Matilda when she married Levi English in 1838. Although Cecelia was not separated from her son, Robert, he was given to Matilda's son, John English. Many slaves already had faced separation when they were brought to Texas while relatives stayed behind. Children of any age might be sold apart from parents if the economic situation dictated such divisions. Probably one-fourth to one-third of all slave families met some form of separation as a result of sales. Slaves responded with tears, said James Brown, "like they at the funeral when they am parted, they has to drag them away." Others tried, sometimes successfully, to gain permission for weekend or holiday visits if the distance was not too great. When the Civil War ended, newly freed slaves often sought to find family members over great distances.[15]

Although a law made marriage between white Americans and African Americans illegal, some slaveholders did form relationships and have families with slave women. In some cases the relationships proved temporary, yet other owners freed the children born to slave mothers and gave them property or helped them to get an education. But such support of black family members did not always happen.[16]

When slaves tried to keep up their spirits under the work demands and controls of slavery, they turned to religion as well as families. Slaveholders allowed slaves to worship in some cases because religion could be used to preach obedience to owners. Owners often encouraged bondsmen to attend nearby white-led congregations.

While slaves in some churches sat in separate pews from whites, more often different services were held on Sundays. Many heard sermons by white ministers. African American preachers led services for black congregations under the observation of white members from the same denomination. At least a few thousand slaves became members of predominantly white denominations, with the Methodists and the Baptists claiming the largest numbers, followed by the Presbyterians, Episcopalians, Catholics, and Disciples of Christ. Many slaves held religious meetings in secret where they could speak more freely.

The lessons and messages learned by bondsmen even from the sermons of white ministers ranged beyond obedience and hard work. Mary Gaffney understood the Christian hope of salvation and a life beyond death "where they would not be any more slaves." Others in private or in secret meetings offered prayers for deliverance from bondage. A few may have learned to read because a religious slaveholder believed in Bible reading by all Christians.

Even in Texas, the newest of the slave states, a few slaves were smuggled in directly from Africa, despite a law against bringing slaves from other countries. Among those people, some kept a Muslim faith that involved daily prayers facing east toward Mecca.[17]

Religion joined with family ties to encourage careful burial practices, some with African origins. Slaves brought with them beliefs about scraping all grass away from graves. Furthermore, they began the decoration of gravesites with seashells and broken pieces of pots, practices that also existed among Anglos and Native Americans. Slave craftsmen may have carved some stone grave markers. The burials thus reflected folk art traditons.[18]

Music added another important piece to the black culture under slavery. Some styles of music had connections to African culture. Bondsmen fashioned instruments such as banjos and drums reflecting that heritage. Slaves changed the patterns of white music to fit their own backgrounds. For example, hymns sung in church might take on a more lively rhythm for African Texans. Slaves sang while working to lighten the burden and as a way to control the pace of labor. Music provided a way to let emotions flow more freely. "If he was happy, it [music] made him happy; if he was sad, it made him feel better," remembered Vinnie Brunson. Slaves might sing on Saturday evenings to express joy at the end of a work week or to forget the hardships of labor and punishments.

Songs could have double meanings, especially for slaves secretly trying to escape or learn to read. One bondsman acted as a lookout and began to sing a special tune if an owner or overseer appeared. Millie Ann Smith recalled that Rusk County slaves hummed spirituals while working. "It was our way of praying for freedom," she explained.[19]

Just as music reflected the feelings of slaves, so too did their folklore. Bondsmen remembered and passed on stories from one generation to the next by word of mouth. Tales could show humor while explaining how to deal with slaveholders in awkward situations. The rabbit appeared in African folklore as an important figure. Thus, Brer Rabbit emerged in the South as a trickster figure, representing slaves, who usually outwitted Brer Fox and Brer Bear, who symbolized the more powerful slaveholders. In Texas, Old John, a fictional black man, took on many of the same roles and became the best-known figure in folktales. That approach received clear expression in the words of Harriet Robinson:

Ex-slave Jane Bell stands beside her home in Utley, Texas. She wears a necklace of aspidistra to ward off colds and spirits, c. 1935. Institute of Texan Cultures illustration no. 102-168

▼▼▼

25

In this 1893 photograph of a camp outing, men are seen carrying on the musical traditions of past generations. Institute of Texan Cultures illustration no. 86-443

I fooled Old Master seven years,
Fooled the overseer three.
Hand me down my banjo,
And I'll tickle your bel-lee.[20]

Slaves celebrated the few holidays allowed by owners. The major time of rest began at Christmas and usually continued through New Year's day, a period after harvests had been completed and before the planting season began. Bondsmen might focus on the religious meaning but could also turn to lighter music and dances. Some had a chance to see relatives on nearby farms or go into the nearest town. The Fourth of July provided a briefer holiday in the summer, when slaves joined together to relax and socialize. Celebrating harvests became important to slaves on many large plantations, with the agreement of planters who sometimes attended. Surprisingly the celebration focused, not on the crops grown for sale, but rather on the corn that would feed them and the farm animals.

Harrison Boyd remembered "a big cornshucking every fall." Cato Carter recalled that "a beef was kilt and they'd have a reg'lar picnic feastin'. They was plenty of whiskey . . . jus' like Christmas." "Yes and us had good music, too" added Robert Franklin. As Lu Lee explained: "they hollered out, 'Get your partners fo [*sic*] the ring dance,'" a dance brought from Africa. Folklorist Roger Abrahams explained: "To white onlookers, the event was an entertainment verging on the spectacular; to the slaves, it was an opportunity to celebrate together," in ways that kept alive their African and American heritage.[21]

Slaves hoped for freedom from their controlled status, and the moments when they achieved some measure of freedom became times for celebration. Since the many controls imposed by slaveholders and the state limited the chances of gaining freedom, some bondsmen fought against being punished, which might result in owners killing those slaves. Other slaves found ways to get even with owners who demanded more work than people could do without collapsing. Barns might be burned or tools broken. New possibilities for opposing slavery led groups of slaves to revolt. When the Mexican Army battled the Texans in 1835 during the Texas revolution, bondsmen along the Brazos River planned a revolt. But they were discovered and severely punished. Other slaves on the Colorado River, in 1856, wanted to fight their way to Mexico, only to have owners learn of their hopes, which led to whippings or death sentences.

Thousands of bondsmen did gain their freedom by running away. One owner placed a notice for his escaped slave in the *Houston Telegraph and Texas Register* of February 12, 1845:

> RAN AWAY from the subscriber, a little negro girl, about 8 or 9 years old, light black complexion, named Eliza. She had on a black calico dress when she ran away. A reward of twenty dollars will be given to any person who will deliver this runaway to the subscriber.
>
> *A.EWING*[22]

Some runaways traveled east seeking family members, while others turned north through the Indian Territory (later Oklahoma) to

Kansas, a state where many settlers opposed slavery. The largest number of slaves, however, turned south to Mexico where freedom waited across the Rio Grande. Once they crossed the river they celebrated their success and tried to avoid the men hired by slaveholders to bring them back.[23] In 1845 twenty-five blacks from Bastrop mounted on the best horses they could find supposedly escaped to Mexico. Others were not so successful, such as two escaped slaves that belonged to a Mr. Lott who lived on the San Antonio River. In 1853, they were shot by a group of U.S. soldiers near Brownsville when they refused to surrender. Lott was not pleased about the loss of his most valuable property.

The hope of freedom increased during the Civil War as Union armies advanced into the Confederate states, including Texas, and President Abraham Lincoln issued the Emancipation Proclamation in 1862. Slaves in Texas had less chance of gaining freedom because the Union armies landed only briefly on the Gulf Coast. Yet, some bondsmen did escape to the Union Army or to Union ships near the coast. A greater number found more freedom by staying where they were because with some owners away fighting in the Confederate Army, slaves faced less supervision and control over their daily lives. Slaves in other Confederate states during the war joined the Union Army when the troops arrived. The African American soldiers helped defeat the Confederacy and win freedom for other slaves, including those in Texas. For African Texans emancipation day came on June 19, 1865, when the Union Army under General Gordon Grainger arrived in Galveston. The *Houston Tri-Weekly Telegraph* of June 23, 1865 reported:

> The people of Texas are informed that in accordance with a proclamation from the Executive of the United States, all slaves are free. This involves an absolute equality of personal rights and rights of property, between former masters and slaves, and the connection heretofore existing between them, becomes that between employer and hired labor. The freemen are advised to remain at their present homes, and work for wages. They are informed that they will not be allowed to collect at military posts; and that they will not be supported in idleness either there or elsewhere.[24]

*An engraving of a Union
Army soldier, an escaped
slave, that appeared in*
Harper's Weekly, *July 2,
1864.* Institute of Texan
Cultures illustration no.
75-1385

Juneteenth, commemorating the end of slavery in Texas, is celebrated in San Antonio's Alamo Plaza, c. 1900s. Institute of Texan Cultures illustration no. 86-400

Slaves celebrated. "Everyone was singing," recalled Felix Haywood. "We was all walking on golden clouds," even though some former slaveholders threatened violence to stop the expressions of happiness. Yet the celebrations would continue, as June 19 became known as Juneteenth, a day to remember the importance of freedom.[25]

CHAPTER 3
Life after Emancipation

ONCE AFRICAN AMERICANS in Texas became free people they developed goals that tried to overcome the severe limitations of slavery. Black Texans wanted to shape their own families, use their economic skills to help themselves, create schools for the education of their children, form their own churches, and control their own social and cultural lives, all within a society that was to allow them equal opportunity and legal status.

To reach these goals black people urged that laws should no longer limit their place or roles in society. They wanted the right to vote for political leaders who made decisions about laws that could advance or restrict their progress. Because of white majorities in the state legislature and in the United States Congress, decisions on legal and political status depended on finding some Anglo Americans who favored greater equality.

In the years immediately after the Civil War, the late 1860s, a majority in the U.S. Congress, who had opposed secession and favored national unity, also passed laws and constitutional amendments that made African Americans citizens of the United States with the right to vote. Yet other white Americans and Texans, who had favored the old slave system, opposed those laws and threatened or attacked African Americans who voted or used the other rights of citizens. Despite the problems, in 1868, African American voters helped elect a Republican majority to a constitutional convention that included nine black delegates. In 1869, a similar majority was elected to the legislature, including fourteen African

William Madison McDonald (1866–1950)

William Madison McDonald achieved a variety of goals when he became a prominent leader in African American fraternal organizations, business, and politics. He was born in Kaufman County, Texas, on June 22, 1866. Working part-time for an attorney-rancher allowed him to complete high school and study at Roger Williams University in Tennessee. In the 1880s and early 1890s, he taught school and helped to organize a black state fair in North Texas. During that period, he took an active role in African American fraternal groups, beginning with the Seven Stars of Consolidation of America. He rose quickly to be its Supreme Grand Chief by 1889. By that time, he also had accepted membership in the

C. W. Bryant, a delegate from Harris County to the Texas Constitutional Convention, 1868–69. Institute of Texan Cultures illustration no. 76-67

▼▼▼

Lizzie Brown, a resident of Waelder, Texas, poses with umbrella and fan for this studio portrait, c. 1890s. Institute of Texan Cultures illustration no. 80-251

Prince Hall Free and Accepted Masons. In 1892, he aided the formation of the Hero-ines of Jericho. Those groups reflected the views of an emerging black middle class that promoted leadership, economic development, efforts to retain political and civil rights, and community social life.

McDonald began to work for the Masons in 1890, and by 1899 had risen to the Right Worshipful Grand Secretary, the powerful, day-to-day director, and held that position for fifty years. Under his leadership the Texas Masons created a cotton mill, published a maga-zine, offered insurance to members, and estab-lished a bank in Fort Worth that he managed. He developed at least temporary support for the Fraternal Bank and Trust from other African American fraternal groups. With him as

▼▼▼

director it survived the Great Depression of the 1930s.

McDonald, with the aid of white business-man E. H. R. Green, rose to prominence in the state Republican Party of the 1890s and attended some national conventions as leader of the Black and Tan faction in Texas into the 1920s. His death came on July 4, 1950.

Source: Bruce A. Glasrud, "William M. McDonald: Business and Fraternal Leader," in *Black Leaders,* ed. by Barr and Calvert, pp. 83–112; Tyler and Barnett, eds., *New Handbook of Texas,* v. 4, p. 393.

First African American public school in San Antonio, c. 1877–78. Institute of Texan Cultures illustration no. 78-54

American legislators. The new black political leaders included ministers, teachers, farmers, blacksmiths, and other skilled craftsmen. Efforts by African Texans and some white Texans, usually Unionists, to have the state control the violence against black people and provide schools for all citizens proved unpopular with others who generally had supported the Confederacy.[1]

Discrimination continued against black Texans such as that experienced in 1886 by "Bones" Hooks in the town of Wamba near Texarkana. Hooks had saved some money and invested it in a grocery store. He arrived one day, eighteen months later, to find a sign on the door that said, "We give you thirty-six hours to get out." The White Caps of Sand Gall Gizzard signed it. To escape some of the pressures from this continuing discrimination by whites, and to promote jobs, groups of African Texans established at least fifty black or predominantly black communities during the late 1800s. These villages, such as Germany near Crockett, usually formed a social center for surrounding farms and farm workers. Sympathetic whites provided land in a few cases, while some African Texans saved money to buy land to start more communities. Peyton Colony in Blanco

County developed soon after emancipation and took its name from an early guiding figure, Peyton Roberts. Kendleton in Fort Bend County emerged from white-black cooperation on land sales in 1884. Some of the villages had a religious focus, such as St. John Colony near Lockhart, where John Henry Winn, a minister, provided leadership in its formation. Cologne in Goliad County emerged as a trade center soon after the Civil War. A railroad stimulated the development of the Cologne community in the 1880s by creating a depot especially for cattle shipping.[2]

More black Texans began to move into the larger towns of the state once they gained the freedom to travel. They chose to live in urban areas because the towns offered a greater range of jobs, less threat of violence from the Ku Klux Klan and similar groups, better schools, and more diverse social life. As a result the number of blacks in Texas cities doubled between 1865 and 1870. The black population percentage varied, however, from 40 percent in Houston to 16 percent in San Antonio, and remained about the same in most towns from 1870 to 1900.[3] Concentrations of African Americans at the edges of towns in the 1800s developed into black neighborhoods such as Clarksville in Austin, Tenth Street District in Dallas, and Freedmen's Town in Houston, with several considered historic districts within the expanding cities by the end of the twentieth century.[4]

African Texans grew in number from almost 400,000 in 1880 to 620,000 by 1900. This resulted from the large families during the late nineteenth century and also because of the migration of African Americans from nearby southern states. Yet the hopes that led black people to move into towns also caused other black Texans to consider migration out of the state. In 1879–80, a few thousand African Texans joined the black migration to Kansas. Richard Allen and other black leaders in Texas suggested moves to parts of West Texas where settlement had just begun. The 1880 census indicates there were fifty-one African Texans living in the Panhandle, including a small community of twenty-three persons at Mobeetie. Other African Americans in the state chose to enter Oklahoma when that territory was opened to settlement in the 1890s, and some moved to

Robert Lloyd Smith (1861–1943)

During the late nineteenth and early twentieth centuries, Robert Lloyd Smith made himself a leading spokesman for black economic development, especially in agriculture and education. He was born in Charleston, South Carolina, during 1861. As the son of a free black family, he received an education that included study at the University of South Carolina and graduation from Atlanta University. About 1880, he moved to Texas and by 1885 served as principal for Oakland Normal School in Colorado County.

He became a supporter of economic education, with connections to Booker T. Washington, and a member of the board for the Jeannes Fund that aided black schools. He created the Farmers

Home Improvement Society in 1890 to urge land ownership by black farmers. The society promoted cooperative buying and aid to members, which soon attracted additional supporters in neighboring states. Its activities expanded to include a college with agriculture courses and a bank at Waco.

As a representative in the Texas legislature during the 1890s he favored improvements for the state-supported Prairie View Normal School. While serving as a deputy U.S. Marshal in the early twentieth century he also started a business that made overalls. Members of the new National Negro Business League in 1907 chose him as the president for the Texas chapter. When county extension programs developed in Texas by 1915, he directed the Negro Division to aid

the black towns in Oklahoma such as Langston. Smaller groups considered emigration to Mexico or to Liberia in Africa, but only limited numbers left the state in the 1890s.[5]

Most black Texans worked to achieve their economic independence and raise their families within the state. After slavery ended they could work for pay or, in farming, they could become sharecroppers. Probably most black farmers chose sharecropping because it gave them more control over how they farmed, with less supervision that might remind them of the controls under slavery. People rented land and primarily raised cotton, then shared the crop with the landowner. In good years their labor led to a profit for both the sharecropper and the landowner. Yet poor crops often resulted from lack of rain, floods, or insect problems. Many freedmen, who as slaves had often worked the fields in large supervised groups raising crops, used their farming skills on their own family-sized plots of rented land, hoping to save money and buy small farms for themselves. By 1880, the United States census showed that almost 20 percent of black Texas farmers had bought small farms in several counties.[6]

Well into the twentieth century African American farmers used their skills to build their own cabins or larger houses and to make their own furniture. Women used their abilities in sewing and dy-

A settler hauls a wagonload of cotton with a team of horses, c. 1910. Institute of Texan Cultures illustration no. 75-297

▼▼▼

Bill Pickett bulldogging at Burdick, Kansas, 1915. Institute of Texan Cultures illustration no. 75-586

African Americans in agriculture. He died in Waco on July 10, 1942.

Source: Tyler and Barnett, eds., *New Handbook of Texas,* v. 5, pp. 1108–1109.

ing cloth to make clothes for their families. About half of the women planted gardens to feed their families, while over three-fourths raised chickens for eggs to eat and sell. Two-thirds of the women helped their husbands in the fields at planting and harvest times. Thus, black farm families often became self sufficient, if they could raise food crops and chickens or pigs as well as a crop to be sold, usually cotton.[7]

A smaller group of black Texans worked as cowboys when they chose their own way to earn a living after emancipation. Some of them continued to herd cattle on the gulf coastal plains as they had before the Civil War. Monroe Brackens received his wages for catching wild horses and "breaking" them. A cowboy who worked in Fort Bend County, Bob Jones, saved his pay and within a few years had bought forty cattle as well as five horses. Louis Power served as foreman for the Duke division on the O'Connor ranches near Goliad in the early twentieth century. While most cowboys, black and white, were men, "Aunt Rittie" Williams Foster herded cattle while riding a horse bareback in the Refugio area. She had a variety of skills, however, for she also acted as a midwife helping other women give birth.[8]

William Pickett (1870–1932)

Bill Pickett developed from a fine cowboy in Central Texas into a nationally known rodeo star of the early twentieth century. He was born William Pickett on December 5, 1870, in Travis County. He attended school through the fifth grade and then turned to work, as the second child among thirteen brothers and sisters.

After acquiring skills for handling horses and cattle, he created an unusual form of bull-dogging steers. He could wrestle one down by clamping his teeth into the steer's upper lip. That daring style won him money at exhibitions and fairs in the region. He and his brothers broke horses for a living at Taylor in Central Texas, where he married Maggie Turner in 1890 and attended a Baptist church.

Other black cowboys became drovers who helped take cattle up the trails to railroads and markets on the central Great Plains. Ben Kinchlow remembered: "I went up the trail five or six times" to Kansas and the Dakotas. On those drives he dealt successfully with problems from freezing rain and stampedes to rattlesnakes and got the cattle through each time. Shanghai Pierce, a noted rancher of the gulf coast region, assigned his long-time black cowboy Neptune Holmes to carry his gold on drives and cattle-buying trips. Jim Kelly rode for Print Olive, who gathered a herd in Williamson County for a drive north. In Ellsworth, Kansas, Kelly shot a gambler who had attacked Olive over a card game in a saloon. The Matthews family developed ranches in Shackelford County and drove cattle up the trail to Colorado and Montana. One of their best hands, Bill "Tige" Avery, worked as a skilled roper and bronc rider.[9] African Americans who became cowboys generally faced less discrimination in pay than other black workers.

As cattlemen moved into West Texas, some African American cowboys joined that migration. Bose Ikard worked on the ranch of the white Ikard family in Parker County before the Civil War. After the conflict he joined Charles Goodnight who developed cattle trails to New Mexico and Colorado from West Texas. In his work with Goodnight, Ikard fought off Indian raids and headed off stampedes. On the XIT ranch in the Panhandle–South Plains, Jim Perry proved himself an able roper and bronc rider. As he grew older he became a fine chuck wagon cook for the younger cowboys during the cattle roundups. At other times, he hauled supplies in a freight wagon to the line camps. He commented in later years on the racial limits of the times: "If it weren't for my damned old black face I'd have been boss of one of these divisions long ago."

George Adams moved in a different direction, from South Texas to the Trans-Pecos region. There he worked on the 7D ranch and later for C. F. Cox, Sr., out of Sanderson. He tamed wild horses and herded cattle, sometimes taking his pay in cows instead of money. Many persons believed Addison Jones to be the finest African American cowboy in West Texas. He worked for George W. Littlefield on

Cowboy George "7D" Adams on his horse "Baquet." Institute of Texan Cultures illustration no. 98-613

He traveled across Texas and several western states to rodeos and first won national recognition at the Cheyenne Frontier Days in 1904. The following year he joined the 101 Ranch of Oklahoma, which operated a traveling Wild West Show that also included Will Rogers and Tom Mix. Tours took him across the country to New York City, to the Calgary Stampede in Canada, and to Mexico City, as well as to Argentina, Brazil, and London, England, during the first three decades of the twentieth century.

Although limited by segregation, he participated with great skill in some rodeo events, and at times was identified as an Indian since he probably did have some Native American ancestry. He also played parts in two western movies.

▼▼▼

A horse kicked him in a ranch accident and he died on April 2, 1932. He later received recognition by the National Cowboy Hall of Fame and the U.S. Postal Service put his image on a stamp.

Source: Tyler and Barnett, eds., *New Handbook of Texas*, v. 5, p. 191; Bailey C. Hanes, *Bill Pickett, Bulldogger* (Norman: University of Oklahoma Press, 1977).

the LFD ranch, where his range of skills included "topping off" or taming wild horses and roping with uncanny accuracy. He also directed the work of other black cowboys and often had responsibility for training younger white cowboys, but he never worked as the crew boss for mixed white and black crews. An impressive memory for horses and brands added to his reputation, which even found its way into a song entitled "Whose Old Cow."[10]

The career of Mathew "Bones" Hooks reflected changes in the twentieth century. He began as a bronc rider, taming horses from Wichita Falls to the Panhandle. After riding on some trail drives he became an expert horse handler who sometimes cared for the *remuda* of horses on a ranch. When barbwire fencing closed the open range and the railroads crossed the state, the need for cowboys declined in the early 1900s, so Hooks began to work in towns for hotels and on the railroads. In Clarendon and later Amarillo he became a leader in the black community, establishing churches, parks, and boys clubs.[11]

Daniel Webster Wallace probably became the most financially successful of the black cowboys. From an early job on the Nunn ranch he moved on to the Mann ranch near Abilene in the 1870s. Wallace used part of his pay to buy cattle and land in Mitchell County of West Texas. Despite going broke once and trailing his herd to New Mexico to survive a drought, he rebuilt his ranch to nine thousand acres in the early twentieth century and played an active role in a local church as well as a school. Installing one of the earliest windmills in the area helped him survive future droughts.[12]

Black soldiers as well as cowboys became examples of African Americans gaining jobs in which they acquired new skills. Black men who joined the army on the western frontier received better pay than most jobs offered in the late nineteenth century. While serving in the military they developed practical abilities in horsemanship and handling weapons, as well as survival skills. The U.S. Army formed four regiments of black soldiers after the Civil War, following the pattern of segregated service that developed for African American volunteers during that conflict. The Ninth and Tenth

Cavalry and the Twenty-fourth and Twenty-fifth Infantry all served in West Texas or along the Rio Grande border with Mexico. From Indians they received the respectful nickname of Buffalo Soldiers. Black ministers who served as chaplains for the regiments also taught schools, which allowed many of the soldiers to gain a basic education.

Among the twenty-three African American troopers who won the Congressional Medal of Honor from 1870 to 1898, five performed those acts of leadership and courage while stationed in Texas. Emanuel Stance, a sergeant in the Ninth Cavalry, earned the first Medal of Honor leading a patrol from Fort McKavett in May, 1870. The Buffalo Soldiers hunted Apaches who had stolen horses and taken two boys from a nearby farm. The Stance patrol recaptured several horses and caused the Indians to free one captive as they retreated. The following day Stance and his men drove off Indians trying to seize army horses. This success, which followed earlier ones, led to a Medal of Honor for "gallantry" and "good judgment."[13]

Another group of black soldiers from a different background received the title Seminole Negro Indian Scouts. Their parents had

The ranch home of Mr. and Mrs. Daniel "80 John" Webster Wallace near Loraine, Texas, c. 1935. Institute of Texan Cultures illustration no. 73-1223

▼▼▼

41

The African American Twenty-fifth Infantry was composed of enlisted men, c. 1883. Institute of Texan Cultures illustration no. 68-1045

Eight African American members of the "A" troop of the Tenth Cavalry, c. 1890. Institute of Texan Cultures illustration no. 75-299

lived with the Seminole Indians in Florida, where many of the African Americans in the Carolinas and Georgia had run away to escape slavery. With the Seminoles they had fought in the 1830s and 1840s against forced removal to present-day Oklahoma, but later they agreed to migrate if they could keep their freedom. Fear of being enslaved again or dominated by Creek Indians in Oklahoma Territory caused some African Americans and Seminoles to move into Mexico until after the Civil War. At the request of the U.S. military, some of the Black Seminoles returned to Texas after the war and enlisted as Indian scouts for the army. They usually operated from Fort Clark in South Texas with their families living in nearby Brackettville. In the 1870s and 1880s, they served with twenty-six expeditions and received four Medals of Honor. As one of four scouts who held off twenty-five Comanches during the Red River War of 1874, Adam Paine became the first to be honored for "habitual courage" and "cool daring."

The following year, three scouts and their white lieutenant, John L. Bullis, engaged a group of about thirty Comanches near the Pecos River. Outnumbered, they pulled back but Bullis could not reach his horse to remount. Under fire from the Comanches, Sgt. John Ward on horseback rescued Bullis, while trumpeter Isaac Payne and Pvt. Pompey Factor returned fire to cover them. All three scouts received Medals of Honor. Historian Kevin Mulroy concluded that "the black scouts had displayed courage, loyalty, and quickness of wit in completing a remarkable rescue."[14]

Fort Concho National Historic Landmark and Museum at San Angelo provides excellent exhibits on Buffalo soldiers. The Seminole-Negro Indian Scout Cemetery near Fort Clark at Brackettville includes the graves of several black Seminole men who earned Medals of Honor.[15]

While most African Texans after emancipation pursued their lives in various rural occupations, those who had moved into the growing towns of Texas sought to use existing skills or to learn new trades. Some worked in lumbering communities throughout East Texas. Most blacks found less skilled work or dangerous jobs that white people wanted to avoid. Yet other African American men found work as blacksmiths, bricklayers, or painters. To help support families, more black women labored than did white women because black men were often not paid enough to sustain a family. Those women found jobs as laundresses, house servants, cooks, and nursemaids caring for children. Anna Crenshaw Hooks found work washing and ironing linens at the Elmhurst Hotel in Colorado City when it opened.

▼▼▼

Black Seminole scout John Jefferson poses in his army uniform. Institute of Texan Cultures illustration no. 68-932

▼▼▼

In 1883, black men under the guidance of Norris Wright Cuney, a political leader, formed a longshoremen's association that worked loading and unloading ships in the Galveston harbor docks. Others became construction workers who helped build the new railroads in Texas and in some cases labored for the rail lines later as porters, ticket punchers, and in other roles.[16] Some became business owners and others skilled tradesmen. Joshua Houston, who had been a slave blacksmith and servant for Sam Houston, established his own blacksmith shop in Huntsville during the late 1860s and emerged as a leader in the African American community of Walker County.[17]

While African Americans in Texas sought new economic opportunities, they also took steps to stabilize and formalize their family situations, which had not been legal under slavery. Couples went to Freedmen's Bureau agents, ministers, and civil officials to have their

Although he never held elective office, Norris Wright Cuney was very prominent in the Texas Republican Party from 1872 to 1892. Institute of Texan Cultures illustration no. 68-939

Domestic workers pose outside a San Antonio residence, c. 1900. Institute of Texan Cultures illustration no. 85-74

marriages made legal. In many cases, African Americans tried to locate relatives from whom they had been separated during slavery. Others formed new marriages of their own choosing because their former slaveholders had pressured them into unwanted relationships to increase the number of slave children.

Black parents opposed a new apprenticeship law that allowed local officials to take children away and assign them to work for a white family. Free African American men could legally defend their wives from being molested by white men, although such actions usually produced violence. Black women tried to stay home with new babies and small children longer than they had been allowed to under slavery. As men earned wages after emancipation they felt new pride in the ability to take care of their families. The U.S. census in 1870 showed that 80 percent or more of black families included both father and mother, whether the family lived in rural counties such as Matagorda, Smith, and Grayson, or in a large town like Galveston.[18]

African Americans formed new families after a courting period that often began as young people met and got to know each other while walking long distances to rural schools. Others met at work if their families sharecropped on neighboring farms where sons and daughters helped with planting and harvesting. Weddings followed formal introductions to parents. Ceremonies usually came after a church service on Sunday, to avoid conflict with work. After marriage, a husband and wife might share a house with another young couple because neither could afford to rent the house on their own. Mothers also assisted each other in caring for the children.[19]

Black families confirmed their status as free people and their identity by legalizing surnames (last names), which had not received that level of recognition under slavery. Some kept the family names of slaveholders for easier recognition. When Bob was set free at seventeen years of age with no last name, he had trouble deciding on a last name, so the owner of the ranch where he worked, Duncan

Five waiters at the Shell Hotel in Rockport, Texas, August, 1893. Institute of Texan Cultures illustration no. 86-380

Richard H. Boyd
(1843–1922)

Richard Henry Boyd rose from slavery to become a leader in the National Baptist Convention formed by African American Baptists after the Civil War. Boyd was born to a slave mother in Mississippi on March 5, 1843, and named Dick Gray. In 1849, planter B. A. Gray moved him to work in Washington County, Texas. During the Civil War, Boyd acted as a personal servant for Gray until the slaveholder died fighting in Tennessee. Then Boyd brought home a wounded son of the planter and began to manage Gray's cotton plantation. When freedom came at the end of the conflict, he found work as a cowboy and later in a lumber mill. He legalized his name, Richard Henry Boyd, in 1867, as he taught himself to read

Lemons, took him to Eagle Pass and gave Bob his last name. Bob became Robert Lemons and lived out his life in Dimmit County. Others adopted names of symbolic importance such as Lincoln or Free or Liberty.

White Texans and other southerners encouraged legislators to adopt laws against intermarriage between blacks and whites, yet some white men continued to force themselves on black women, especially servants who might lose jobs if they refused. Other white men lived with black women in more affectionate relationships, although the couples could not marry. Children born to these couples added to the population of mixed ancestry. Yet only a small number of light-skinned persons tried to pass as white. Most mulattoes (persons of white and black ancestry) faced the same limitations in their lives as other African Americans.[20]

An example of the complex ancestry for some Texans appeared in the life of Louis Power, a grandson of James Power, the founder of an Irish colony in Mexican Texas during the 1820s. Louis was the son of James Power, Jr., and an African American mother. He grew up on the large O'Connor ranch in Refugio County where he rose to division boss, or foreman, during the first half of the twentieth century. But during that period he could never expect to be treated as an equal by either the whites or the blacks.

The Payne family of the Big Bend area reflected another variation in the patterns of mixed ancestry. Antonia Payne came from the black Seminole group that had migrated with some Seminoles from Florida to the Indian Territory and later Mexico. In Mexico she married Natividad Mariscal, a man of Mexican ancestry who later came to the United States and joined the black Seminole army scouts. One of their sons, Monroe Payne, reached manhood in Mexico but later moved to the Big Bend area in Texas. There he worked as a cowboy, ranch foreman, occasional bootlegger, and freighter who owned cattle and land in the region. His sons also labored as cowboys and foremen on ranches and some married Mexican women in the Big Bend area.[21] Monroe's granddaughter Nora Payne learned of her African ancestry when a local historian

Richard Henry Boyd. Institute of Texan Cultures illustration no. 68-935

and write from basic schoolbooks.

His life changed in important ways during 1869 with his marriage to Hattie Moore and his acceptance as a Baptist preacher. Energetically he formed a regional Baptist convention with six African American congregations. In the Missionary Baptist Convention of Texas, he accepted duties as its secretary and as its superintendent of missions for the state. He continued to lead in founding new congregations for East Texas towns such as Crockett and Navasota, as well as one in San Antonio.

Boyd, in 1896, accepted election as secretary of home missions for the National Baptist Convention, which included most black Baptists. He then relocated to Nashville, Tennessee, where he established the convention's publishing

told her while she was a student at Sul Ross State University that her grandfather had been a Seminole scout. The family had become completely integrated into the Mexican community of Alpine.

As free people, African Americans in Texas took control of their religious practices as well as their family life. Most of them left white-dominated churches to end the separate, segregated seating and white supervision and to develop their own religious leaders. The new black congregations usually became Baptist or joined one of four Methodist denominations. The northern Methodist Episcopal Church had both black and white congregations, but the other three groups remained entirely African American. They included the African Methodist Episcopal Church and the African Methodist Episcopal Zion Church, both formed in the North before the Civil War, and the Colored (later Christian) Methodist Episcopal Church that developed in the South following the conflict.

A black Baptist State Convention formed in the 1870s, followed by the National Baptist Convention in the 1880s. Smaller numbers of African Americans became Presbyterians, Episcopalians, or Catholics. The new congregations emerged as community centers for black people, with the buildings being used as schools during weekdays, as well as for political and social events on week nights. Clergy often provided leadership for other activities in addition to religious guidance. Some stood among the earliest group of Texas black legislators, who opposed violence and promoted equal legal status and public education. In a survey during the 1990s, Clyde McQueen found 375 active black congregations across the eastern half of the state that began in the nineteenth century. More black churches in Texas have received state or national historical markers than any other type of African American historical site in the state.[22]

Jacob Fontaine provides one example of a minister who began his ministry in the first generation after emancipation. He came to Texas as a slave in 1850 and preached in the separate service for bondsmen at the First Baptist Church in Austin. After freedom, he worked as a caretaker for the state land office. Later he became at different times a grocer, an educator, and the operator of a laundry. But throughout the late nineteenth century he served as a clergyman for black Baptist congregations in Austin. The African American members of the white-led First Baptist Church began in 1867 to hold separate meetings and formed a black First Baptist congregation. Fontaine ministered to the new church for almost twenty years and supervised construction of its first building, completed in 1868. The previous year he had helped create the St. John Regular Missionary Baptist Association with eleven congregations for which he served as the original moderator.

Through the 1870s and 1880s he played a key role in the formation of five more Missionary Baptist congregations in Central Texas. To offer advice to African Americans and meet community needs, Fontaine edited a newspaper, *The Gold Dollar.*

▼▼▼

The African Methodist Episcopal Church in San Antonio, c. 1887. Institute of Texan Cultures illustration no. 91-70

The gold dollar is the name of this little Paper. Its name taken from a gold dollar which was presented to me by my sister Nelly Miller on a visit to Mississippi in 1872 as we had been seppareted [*sic*] by the evel [*sic*] of Slavery for twenty years this gold dollar have traded with since that time and made sixty dollars of it with which I have bought this little Office and started this little paper.

Rev. Jacob Fontaine[23]

As a role model, he registered to vote, aided the establishment of a fraternal group, and spoke at Juneteenth celebrations. The building where he published *The Gold Dollar* and one of the churches he founded remain as historical landmarks in Austin.[24]

Folk tales about preachers became a strong theme in black folklore following the Civil War. Because public schools for African

The choir and band of the New Hope Baptist Church in Waco, Texas, c. 1912. Institute of Texan Cultures illustration no. 68-1023

Americans began only after emancipation, verbal folklore or storytelling remained more common than written literature in the late nineteenth century. The patterns of the usually amusing tales ranged from comments on race relations to farm and ranch life as well as ghost stories. J. Mason Brewer, a nationally known African American folklorist of Texas, explained that the "tales, although humorous in nature, should not convey the idea that the . . . preacher and his followers were showmen or that they did not take their religion seriously." Instead, as in the folklore of other ethnic groups, important leaders become the focus of "witty stories told by . . . followers." In one story the ghosts of a former preacher and church members frightened away new ministers. Finally a new preacher spoke in a sermon to the ghosts urging them to tithe, or offer 10 percent of their wealth, to the church. Rather than contribute, the ghosts fled the building, which allowed the living members to return and worship.

Brewer's preservation of regional dialect and black folktales has contributed much to the literature of African Texans, as in the case of a man's prayer asking to be saved from an alligator in the Brazos River: "Gawd, Ah knows youse got a habit of sen'in' yo' son down heah to do yo' work, but Ah wanna tell you rat now, don' you come sen'in' yo' son down heah now, you come down heah you'se'f, caze savin' me from dis alluhgattuh is a man's job."[25]

African American religious denominations and some Anglo groups such as the American Missionary Association established schools after the Civil War to provide educational opportunities for blacks. In the late 1860s, church groups aided the federal Freedmen's Bureau in the creation of elementary schools by recruiting and paying teachers and by providing books for students. Teachers instructed children in the daytime, working adults in night classes, and held separate Sunday schools to help people read the Bible.

Many white Texans opposed educational efforts for the African Americans because they saw education as a threat to Anglo control of labor. They refused to house or sell supplies to teachers and burned some schools. Nevertheless, between 1866 and 1870 the Freedmen's Bureau, with the aid of religious organizations and local black families, founded almost one hundred schools that taught over five thousand students as early as 1867. The enrollments varied because of the need for children to help during the planting or harvesting seasons on farms and because of a yellow fever epidemic.

J. Mason Brewer, a writer of African American folk literature, working at home. Institute of Texan Cultures illustration no. 73-1719

The original sewing class of St. Philip's College in San Antonio, in the spring of 1898. Institute of Texan Cultures illustration no. 74-1227

The Freedman's Bureau and the churches together began the process of finding or training educated African Americans who could become teachers and help expand the number of schools for their children. Several of these instructors proved themselves successful leaders in black communities and later won election to local offices or to the state legislature. W. H. Holland, who had attended Oberlin College in Ohio, later instructed students in Austin and then as a state representative introduced the proposal for the first state-supported black college, Prairie View.[26]

A Republican majority in the state convention of 1868–69 wrote a new state constitution that called for an expanded public school system and, for the first time, the inclusion of African Americans. Because of some Anglo opposition, the legislature allowed local officials to decide whether the new schools would be integrated or segregated. To gain support for the new school system from the white majority in the state, local boards chose to develop separate schools. The interest in education proved strong among African Americans who, by the early 1870s, sent almost fifty thousand black students to the state public schools. Many of the new classes met in churches or other buildings due to the lack of state or local funds to construct new segregated buildings.

▼▼▼

When Democrats won a majority in the legislature, they shifted more power to local officials, who in many areas did not support the black schools and moved toward providing fewer funds per pupil for African Americans. Yet both the black and white population continued to grow in Texas, which resulted in an increased number of African American and Anglo students and schools. To promote progress for black schools, African American teachers in 1884 formed their own Teachers State Association of Texas, because they could not join the white teachers' organization.[27]

W. H. Holland, an African American Texas legislator who introduced a bill creating the first state-supported black college, Prairie View A&M College. Institute of Texan Cultures illustration no. 68-1036

Mary E. Branch (1881–1944)

Mary Elizabeth Branch led the development of Tillotson College in Austin as its president. Her parents' desire to educate their children sparked her own commitment to teaching. She was born the daughter of former slaves in Virginia on May 20, 1881. There she studied at a school in Farmville and later graduated from high school at Virginia State College in Petersburg. After instructing elementary students about English in Blackstone, she began teaching at Virginia State College.

Summer school studies led to her B.A. degree in 1922 from the University of Chicago, where she earned an M.A. degree three years later. In 1927, she joined the social studies faculty of Sumner Junior College at Kansas City,

Mary Elizabeth Branch, president of Tillotson College. Institute of Texan Cultures illustration no. 68-1031

As state and local government assumed support and supervision of elementary schools, religious denominations shifted their attention to the founding of colleges. Colleges had two main goals: the education of black teachers for the public schools and the training of ministers for the religious denomination that supported specific colleges. Some graduates entered other fields, however, and the increased number of college graduates helped to develop a black middle class.

Paul Quinn College in Austin emerged first among these schools in 1872, as the creation of the African Methodist Episcopal Church. After only a few years the college moved to Waco, where more land was acquired and course offerings were expanded. Wiley College opened its doors in 1873 in Marshall, with support from the Freedmen's Aid Society in the Methodist Episcopal Church. In Austin, Tillotson College received a charter in 1877 and held classes first in 1881, under the direction of the American Missionary Association.

This growing group of schools was expanded in 1881 with the founding of Bishop College in Marshall, through the efforts of the white-led Baptist Home Mission Society. The statement of purpose for Bishop College in the 1882 catalog reflected its religious backing: "No system of education can properly be considered complete that does not provide for religious culture. Bishop College has a distinctly religious design, which is kept steadily in view in the daily educational work. It is desired that they who come to receive the benefits of the school, should not only acquire a thorough education in secular knowledge, but that they should leave it intelligent, sensible and earnest Christian men and women."[28]

Guadalupe College became the second Baptist school in 1884, supported by the black Guadalupe Baptist Association, which located the school in Seguin. A college for black women, Mary Allen Seminary, came into being in 1886 at Crockett through the efforts of the Presbyterian Church, U.S.A. Texas College near Tyler received its direction and financial aid from the Colored Methodist Episcopal Church (CME) beginning in 1894. The Episcopal Church supported

Kansas. The following year she moved to St. Louis where she served as dean of women for Vashon High School, a large and important institution for African American girls.

Mary Branch came to Austin, Texas, in 1930 at the request of the American Missionary Society to lead Tillotson College as its president. She reversed a trend toward fewer students and returned the temporary junior college to recognition as a four-year college. During her fourteen years as president she recruited additional faculty, raised money for new buildings, modernized the courses and student programs, and sought to unite Tillotson and Samuel Huston colleges, which occurred later and created a single stronger college.

Beyond her educational efforts, she served as a leader in the local

branch of the National Association for the Advancement of Colored People and as a member of the state Interracial Commission. She also became a member of the Negro Advisory Board for the National Youth Administration in Texas during the Depression. Creation of the United Negro College Fund attracted her active support in the months prior to her death on July 6, 1944.

Source: Olive D. Brown and Michael R. Heintze, "Mary Branch: Private College Educator," in *Black Leaders*, ed. by Barr and Calvert, pp. 112-27; Tyler and Barnett, eds., *New Handbook of Texas*, vol. 1, pp. 700-701.

its only black school, St. Philip's College in San Antonio, which began to accept students in 1898. Samuel Huston College at Austin emerged in 1900 as the second school supported by the Methodist Episcopal Church, after efforts began in 1876 to acquire land and construct buildings. The second Baptist school supported by a regional African American group, the East Texas Baptist Association, appeared in 1905 as Butler College. Jarvis Christian College added the final name to the list of private African American colleges in Texas. The Disciples of Christ created the school at Hawkins in 1912. Some other schools adopted the name *college* but remained high schools. The creation of Guadalupe and Butler colleges reflected tensions that also existed in other black schools over the direction of a college based on white funding.

These eleven colleges received their names from prominent fundraisers or educators in the various religious denominations. Most of the colleges focused on a liberal arts education to develop leaders. St. Philip's varied from this pattern with a vocational orientation, though others offered some similar courses. All of them provided instruction at the elementary and high school levels to prepare students for college courses, since many public schools only offered beginning elementary classes for African Americans.[29]

The state government, in 1878, established Prairie View, the only public college for African Americans until well into the twentieth century. It focused on teacher education as well as some vocational training in agricultural and mechanical subjects. It was attached to Texas A&M College (now Texas A&M University) for administrative purposes. By the late twentieth century historically black colleges and schools ranked second only to churches in receiving recognition as historic sites.[30]

Support for education became a major goal over several generations in many black families. Joshua Houston, the blacksmith and former slave of Sam Houston, helped the Freedmen's Bureau establish a school at Huntsville in the late 1860s. One of his sons attended Prairie View soon after it opened. In the early 1880s, the Huntsville black community, with Joshua Sr. among its leaders, founded Bishop

Monroe A. Majors was an early physician in Texas, 1886. Institute of Texan
Cultures illustration no. 68-950

Ward Normal and Collegiate Institute, although funding problems
forced its closing in a few years. Joshua sent another son, Samuel W.
Houston, to colleges out of state. Samuel then returned to become a
teacher in Huntsville. Early in the twentieth century he led the creation of Sam Houston Industrial and Training School. Started as a
private high school, it soon became part of the Huntsville School
District with Samuel as principal.[31]

Some of the Texas black colleges established student musical
groups similar to the Fisk College Jubilee Singers, who became nationally known for their presentations of spirituals as a method of
fund raising. African-Texan music after the Civil War continued to
include spirituals in churches, as well as folk music based on work
songs, often called shouts or hollers. But changes appeared with freedom. Black musicians could travel more easily to perform in minstrel shows and receive pay. Some chose not to move about, but
played at local social events, whether at churches, schools, clubs and
societies, or Juneteenth celebrations. Others like Scott Joplin in his

Reuben Shannon Lovinggood was a professor of Latin and Greek at Wiley College and the first president of Samuel Huston College, 1900. Institute of Texan Cultures illustration no. 68-1038

*Scott Joplin began taking
music lessons in Texarkana
when he was 11 years old.*
Institute of Texan Cultures
illustration no. 75-768

youth at Texarkana took lessons at times from various black and white piano or music instructors. That training added an awareness of European marches and ballads as well as the ability to read music and write compositions. While in his teens during the 1880s Joplin brought together his two brothers and two friends in a Texas Medley group that played in communities of Northeast Texas.[32]

A slightly older musician, Charley Willis, broke wild horses on the E. J. Morris ranch in Central Texas and helped drive a herd up the trail to Wyoming in 1871. He, like other cowboys, sang to cattle as a way of calming them and avoiding stampedes. While he learned songs from other cowboys, black and white, Willis may have created what later became one of the most famous cowboy ballads, "Goodbye Old Paint."[33] African Americans contributed to a diverse musical heritage in Texas that included ethnic, religious, social, and work elements.

CHAPTER 4

From Discrimination to Participation during the Twentieth Century

jaxon·02

BLACK TEXANS BEGAN the century facing discrimination in jobs, segregation and exclusion in many public places, and limitations on voting. Those problems had begun in the late nineteenth century and in most cases continued into the middle of the twentieth century.

Most African Americans lost the right to vote because of actions, by the state and political parties, aimed primarily at black voters. White citizens in 1902 adopted a poll tax requirement for voting, despite opposition from racial and political minorities. The Democratic Party added a white primary in 1904, after it had developed earlier in many counties. A "Lily White" movement also rose to leadership in the Republican Party during the early twentieth century. These combined actions reduced black voting from a peak of 100,000 during the 1890s to about 5,000 by 1906. The number of African American voters did expand as their population grew, however, reaching 25,000 by 1920. Still their influence remained limited except in some local elections. Because Texas did not employ the registration laws and literacy tests that were used in most of the Deep South states, limits on voting did not reach the level of near-exclusion that existed in those states.

Violence, which had been used at times to discourage black voting, continued into the twentieth century in the form of lynchings.

Bessie Coleman (1892–1926)

Bessie Coleman wanted to fly. She became the first African American to attain a pilot's license and to entertain as a stunt flyer. After her birth January 26, 1892, in Atlanta, Texas, her family moved to Waxahachie. She picked cotton to help pay family bills while completing high school. Lack of money cut short her attendance at a black college in Oklahoma. Then she entered a beauty school in Chicago and later managed a small café.

Through her career she longed to fly. Meeting rejection from U.S. flight schools because of racial segregation, she went to a flight school in France. The license she received in 1921 made her the world's first black pilot. After more study in Germany she returned to the United States where she became a popular figure doing

"Hangman's Day in Wharton" is the caption on this photograph taken of the execution platform where a crowd is gathered to watch the hanging of two black men, c. February, 1910. Institute of Texan Cultures illustration no. 84-1

Lynchings of African Americans by whites occurred to maintain white social and economic dominance. Most white mobs hanged their victims, but in 1930 lynchers in Sherman set fire to the county courthouse instead. From 1882 to 1927, Texas ranked third in the nation with 370 lynchings of blacks. In 1922 Ethel Ransom, a nurse from Fort Worth, became the Texas director of the national Anti-Lynching Crusaders to fight lynchings and other outrages against black people in Texas.

Under the growing pressure of national attention, lynch mobs across the South declined during the 1920s and disappeared in Texas during the 1930s. The Ku Klux Klan, which had revived in the 1920s, spread to Texas, where anti-black violence formed one aspect of Klan activities. African Americans in Texas experienced most of the same pressures and loss of life from white prejudice that limited the lives of all black southerners.[1]

Another problem of race relations, segregation, had increased during the late nineteenth century in public places such as hotels, theaters, and restaurants, as well as in transportation and state institutions, including schools. Some cities segregated residential areas, beginning with Dallas in 1916. Several towns excluded blacks from parks and libraries or offered separate but unequal facilities in

air shows across the nation. After a crash in 1924 she spent a year regaining her health.

In 1925, she made Houston her base camp for her travels. That summer she performed an exciting exhibition in Houston that led observers to call her "Brave Bess." She spoke often to students, urging them to pursue their dreams, including the possibility of being pilots. On other occasions she spoke out against discrimination. In Florida on April 30, 1926, she crashed and died when her plane failed in a test flight. During the 1930s black pilots organized exhibitions in her honor. Her amazing career led the U.S. Postal Service to issue a postal stamp honoring her in 1995.

Source: Rich, *Queen Bess*; Tyler and Barnett, eds., *New Handbook of Texas*, v. 2, pp. 199–200.

A certificate from the Federation Aeronautique Internationale granted Bessie Coleman a pilot's license in France, June 15, 1921. Institute of Texan Cultures illustration no. 85-323

1888   I AM PLEASED TO ANNOUNCE THAT MY   1908

SANITARIUM

is now open for the benefit of the general public, where all of the most scientific operations are being successfully made, at reasonable prices. For further information, call on or address

Bluitt's Sanitarium

504 COMMERCE STREET   PHONE MAIN 518   DALLAS, TEXAS

An advertisement for the opening of the first hospital for blacks in Texas, which was operated by Dr. Benjamin Rufus Bluitt, 1908. Institute of Texan Cultures illustration no. 68-951

Carter W. Wesley (1892–1969)

Carter Walker Wesley changed his career from a lawyer to a newspaper editor and publisher to a public figure who spoke out in favor of greater equality and opportunity for African Americans. He was born on April 29, 1892, in Houston. He graduated from Fisk University with honors in 1917. In the military he earned the rank of lieutenant, despite problems of discrimination, and served in France with the black 372nd and 370th Infantry regiments during World War I. In the fall of 1918 he led his men in battle and briefly commanded a company.

After the war he received a law degree from Northwestern University in 1922 and became an attorney in Oklahoma for five years. Wesley then returned to Houston and soon invested in the Houston

the early twentieth century.[2] "The one thing that really used to bother me as a little girl was why I couldn't go to the library. The public libraries in Houston became open to black people either during my senior year in high school (1956) or after I had graduated. When it was opened, I walked through every inch of the library. That was my sort of defiance."[3]

African Americans responded to problems of segregation and discrimination in part by focusing on economic and social activities and by creating their own similar organizations. In 1900, half or more of African Americans remained in agriculture. Thirty percent of black farmers in Texas owned some property, usually small farms, which ranked them second among states in the Lower South. The other 70 percent of African American farmers worked as sharecroppers on rented land trying to make a profit but often facing debts. Falling prices for farm crops hurt all farmers, but black tenants faced higher interest charges from some white landowners or merchants. Other black men worked as wage laborers on farms.[4]

A smaller but growing group of African Americans worked in towns, most often in unskilled jobs because many Anglo-led unions and businesses reserved the better positions for whites. In response, African Americans tried to organize their own unions to get more skilled jobs. Often black newspaper editors, such as Clifton

▼▼▼

Richardson, Sr., and Carter Wesley of the Houston *Informer,* and businessmen such as C. W. Rice of Houston, encouraged those efforts. Yet they often disagreed on whether to work with white unions or with business owners. Businessmen in turn often hired black workers if the white unions wanted higher wages. That added to a sense of racial competition for jobs, but opened work for black laborers who otherwise had little chance of being hired.[5]

In the early twentieth century, black longshoremen, skilled in loading and unloading ships in Texas ports, grew in number from about 850 in 1910 to about 3,000 in 1940. With separate unions the number of workers was split evenly between white and black longshoremen. The Galveston union of black longshoremen tried to keep alive their history as the first successful black labor organization in the state and to spread their union to other Texas ports. Interracial cooperation existed at times on the docks, but white-black competition and conflict also occurred.[6]

After emancipation some African Americans found jobs with the railroads being built across the state. Some black workers found

Workers shucking oysters at a plant in Port Lavaca, Texas. Institute of Texan Cultures illustration no. 74-73

Informer, a black newspaper. He eventually became its primary voice as editor and publisher. Wesley supported civil and political rights, working with the National Association for the Advancement of Colored People against the white primary that limited voting and against segregation in public places including colleges. Yet he fought to maintain Texas Southern University, the new state-supported black college in Houston, because it provided expanded opportunities for African Americans to acquire higher education. He engaged in debates with local NAACP leaders such as Lulu White over the best strategy to end discrimination. He died in Houston on November 10, 1969.

Source: Tyler and Barnett, eds., *New Handbook of Texas,* v. 6, p. 884.

positions laying the new lines of track; others helped operate the trains as firemen on the engines or as brakemen on the rail cars. In the passenger trains, African Americans served as porters or waiters in the sleeping and dining cars. At stations they labored as baggage handlers or in maintenance positions. Faced with exclusion from white unions, African Americans in Texas began to form local chapters of the Colored Trainmen of America and the Brotherhood of Sleeping Car Porters in the 1920s and 1930s. Dining car waiters protested a state law that required them to work only under white supervision.[7] Cowboy "Bones" Hooks found employment as a porter with the railroad passing through west Texas when the trail drives ended and the work for cowboys decreased.

Oil discoveries at the beginning of the twentieth century launched a new industry in Texas; black as well as white workers found jobs drilling wells and operating the refineries. To avoid competition for jobs, white oil workers' unions supported the formation of black local unions that would join in strikes for better wages. Yet white foremen often gave black workers the cleanup positions.

The Great Depression of the 1930s stirred more interest in unions and more equal protection under the law against discrimination. In

Workmen tend oxen pulling a railroad car from the main rail line to the commercial district in Seguin. Institute of Texan Cultures illustration no. 90-338

▼▼▼

some towns such as Port Arthur in the 1940s, the police threatened anyone, black or white, who tried to form unions, especially those connected to the new national Congress of Industrial Organizations (CIO). New national laws provided workers with more protection from hostile police action. During World War II African Americans formed 6 percent of workers in Texas refineries, but one Port Arthur refinery included eight hundred blacks among three thousand employees.[8]

The oil industry stimulated a demand for new equipment made of steel, which created new jobs for black and white workers. At Hughes Tool, African Americans held almost one-fourth of the positions. To limit outside influences, Hughes Tool created its own union in 1918 that included a Colored Club. Continued discrimination in skilled positions and wages by the company led to new organizing activity efforts by the CIO during the 1930s depression. That resulted in lively competition into the 1940s between the company union and the CIO for the support of black workers.[9]

The Depression reversed the trend toward better wages in towns

Workers with mule teams used during the construction of roads in the Texas oil fields near Luling, Texas. Institute of Texan Cultures illustration no. 93-197

and led to high unemployment, while it pushed many sharecroppers off the land and into towns. Although some new federal programs offered assistance to African Americans, other agencies did not accept them. Thus the percentage of unemployed blacks was generally higher than the percentage for whites.[10]

In addition to steel products, World War II created a demand for more ships during the 1940s. Shipbuilding expanded in Texas and other coastal states with African Americans forming up to 20 percent of the workers. Companies and white unions, however, kept blacks in less skilled positions, at lower pay, despite certificates that showed some had training and experience as welders. Whites attacked blacks in a race riot at Beaumont in 1943, as they had in Port Arthur during World War I, because of economic and social competition. The federal Fair Employment Practices Commission and the National Labor Relations Board investigated the problems, but could not get companies and white unions to end all discrimination.[11]

To overcome racial discrimination and economic limitations, growing numbers of black southerners began to migrate to northern cities seeking greater opportunities, but more black migrants entered Texas than left between 1910 and 1940. Again the movement of African Americans into Texas began from rural areas to growing towns and cities within the state. The percentage of blacks living in Texas towns rose steadily from 16 percent in 1890 to almost 39 percent by 1930 and to about 75 percent by 1960—one of the highest levels of African American urbanization in the South. As a result, Texas through the twentieth century had as many or more cities with a large black population as any state in the United States.[12]

The concentration of African Americans in Texas towns and cities opened the way for them to develop businesses and to seek a greater variety of jobs. Although fifth nationally in the number of black citizens, Texas ranked fourth in businesses owned by African Americans in 1929. Those business owners ranked first, ahead of black owners in all other states, in total profits.

▼▼▼

A cook at the Riegler Confectionary in San Antonio, c. 1915. Institute of Texan Cultures illustration no. 84-346

▼▼▼

Maud Cuney Hare (1874–1936)

Maud Cuney Hare, the daughter of Norris Wright Cuney, the most prominent African American leader in late-nineteenth-century Texas, became nationally known in literature and music. Born February 16, 1874, she completed studies in Galveston at Central High School during 1890. She then entered the New England Conservatory of Music, where she defended her right to live in a dormitory while pursuing an education in piano.

She became a music instructor at the Texas Deaf, Dumb, and Blind Institute for Colored Youth in Austin. She married J. Frank McKinley in 1898, and lived briefly in Chicago before she divorced and returned to Texas to teach at Prairie View State College.

Then she moved to

African Americans established their own newspapers in most large Texas cities by the early 1900s. Among those papers the editors of the Houston *Informer* and the Dallas *Express* spoke most forcefully for black people living in Texas through much of the century. *Sepia,* a popular magazine, began publication for African Americans in 1947 in Fort Worth. *Sepia* soon had 160,000 readers, making it one of the largest African American magazines in the nation.

The National Negro Business League, established by Booker T. Washington, formed local chapters in Texas cities early in the 1900s and created a state organization by 1907. When the league divided in the 1920s, one group began to develop black chambers of commerce. Antonio Maceo Smith pushed successfully in 1936 for a Texas Negro Chamber of Commerce that drew support from twelve local chambers. Black skilled workers in Texas, whose numbers ranked fifth nationally in 1900, rose steadily to second compared to those in other states by 1950.[13]

Like black business people, black Texans involved in professions such as medicine and law ranked high in numbers, second in 1900 and 1950 compared to other states. The Lone Star Medical, Dental and Pharmaceutical Association grew from its founding in the 1880s to have the most members of any African American medical organization on the state level in the 1920s.[14]

Black colleges graduated additional persons with professional skills, including the growing group of African American writers. Those men and women authored stories, books, and poems for the increasing number of literate blacks. Melvin B. Tolson, professor at Wiley College, became a nationally recognized poet, beginning with his volume *Rendezvous with America* in 1944. Thus more formal written works began to share with verbal folklore the passing on of ideas, values, traditions, and entertainment including humor from one generation to the next.

Sutton Griggs, a Baptist minister in North Texas who later moved to Tennessee, authored a series of novels from 1899 to 1908 that explored the diverse ways that African Americans might respond to problems of discrimination. The leading characters in one book,

A graduating class at Bishop College in Marshall, Texas. Institute of Texan Cultures illustration no. 68-1037

Imperium in Imperio, considered creating a separate black state in the Southwest. In other novels, Griggs presented figures engaged in various forms of protest. Finally, in *Pointing the Way,* he shifted the focus to a view of race relations that accepted cooperation by African Americans with wealthy Anglos who would provide protection against violence from other whites.[15]

Accounts of the history of blacks as well as a guide to etiquette began to be written and published along with literature in the late nineteenth and early twentieth centuries. The book *History of African Methodism in Texas* appeared in 1885 from the pen of H. T. Kealing, a Methodist minister. W. A. Redwine authored *Brief History of the Negro in Five Counties,* describing African American contributions to the region around Tyler, where the volume was published in 1901. In 1913, one of the most talented women from Texas, Maud Cuney Hare, published a volume about her father, *Norris Wright Cuney: A Tribune of the Black People,* which chronicled the lives of her father and others who had been active in political, civic, and labor activities in Galveston. Maud Hare remained in the

Boston where she married William P. Hare in 1906 and became part of the African American intellectual community that included her friend W. E. B. DuBois, the great educator and civil rights advocate. She gave formal music presentations, spoke on black literary topics, and established an integrated music school.

As a writer she wrote a play, Antar of Araby, *and four books, including one about her father in 1913. She also edited three books including a volume of poetry by several authors,* The Message of the Trees *(1918) and a collection of Creole Songs (1921). Her important study of* Negro Musicians and Their Music *(1936) appeared after her death February 13, 1936.*

Source: Hales, *A Southern Family in Black and White;* Tyler and Barnett, eds., *New Handbook of Texas,* vol. 2, p. 447.

John Biggers
(1924–2001)

John Biggers achieved national distinction as an artist and as a college art teacher in the late twentieth century. In the nineteenth century when most African Americans worked long hours in agriculture or in heavy urban labor, few had the opportunity to become artists. By the 1920s, some began to find possibilities for teaching careers in art at various colleges.

John Biggers was born in Gastonia, North Carolina, on April 13, 1924, to a father who taught, preached, and farmed with the aid of John's mother, who also worked as a house servant and laundress. In elementary school he learned to draw animals. At Lincoln Academy he added cabinet making to his experiences. Then at Hampton Institute in Virginia he met his wife, Hazel, and

Northeast where she had been educated and gained fame as a musician and writer of a book and articles on music. Josie Briggs Hall, a teacher from Waxahachie, wrote a book suggesting standards of personal conduct, *Hall's Moral and Mental Capsule for the Economic and Domestic Life of the Negro as a Solution of the Race Problem* in 1905.[16]

By the 1920s and 1930s, J. Mason Brewer began to receive recognition as a leading folklorist who gathered and published black folk tales from Texas. He also edited a volume of poetry by black authors educated in the state. Some of the poems had appeared earlier in newspapers or magazines across the nation. Themes included critiques of racial discrimination and conflicts among African Americans. Other poems touched on religion, as well as romantic and realistic views of daily life. The Harlem Renaissance clearly had shaped the work of several authors at this time. Bernice Love Wiggins, one of the authors, taught school in El Paso and wrote a volume of poetry, *Tuneful Tales,* in 1925.[17]

Photographers joined writers as members of the black middle class who helped preserve the heritage of African Americans. Photography offered business opportunities for those who became most successful. The pictures provide what Alan Govenar has called "portraits of community." One generation of black photographers often taught the next. The number of African American professional photographers in Texas grew from at least seven in 1900 to three times that number by the 1950s. Charles G. Harris photographed African Americans in Houston from 1909 until 1931. By that time, Albert C. Teal had begun his Bayou City studio in 1919 and continued until his death in 1956. Teal also offered instruction in photography at local black colleges. His students Elnora Frazier and Juanita Williams became successful photographers. Other prominent African American photographers included Marion Butts of Dallas from the 1940s to the 1980s, Calvin Littlejohn in Fort Worth during the same period, and Curtis Humphrey who began in Fort Worth and Dallas, but spent the longest part of his career in Tyler, from the 1940s to the 1990s. They produced pictures of middle class individuals that reflect dignity and pride.

▼▼▼

John Biggers. Institute of Texan Cultures illustration no. 68-1001

Photographers also captured on film the protests of the Civil Rights movement. Eugene Roquemore worked in Lubbock from the 1950s to the 1990s. Carl Sidle of Dallas and Earlie Hudnall, Jr., of Houston in the 1970s expanded the range of subjects to include working class people in settings that reflected their fears and the problems of poverty. Elizabeth "Tex" Williams of Houston worked as a Women's Army Corps (WAC) photographer from 1944 to 1970. Often she flew as the only woman on Army Air Force missions to photograph combat techniques. Following the war she worked as a photographer for defense intelligence agencies. As a group, African American photographers contributed much to the preservation of a photographic record for the black communities of Texas.[18]

studied painting in a newly created class. At Pennsylvania State University he completed his B.A. degree, an M.S., and an Ed.D. majoring in art in the 1940s and 1950s.

In 1949, he began a teaching career at Texas Southern University in Houston where he developed the art department. Biggers and a colleague painted murals for institutions in the black community, including the Eliza Johnson Nursing Home, the Blue Triangle Branch of the YWCA, Longshoreman's Local 872, the W. C. Johnson Branch of the Houston Public Library, public schools, buildings at Texas Southern University, and Hampton Institute. Students from the department went on to be teachers of art and artists. Biggers added illustrations for books and, after a trip to Africa, a book of

▼▼▼

drawings, Ananse: The Web of Life in Africa, *published in 1962.*

His art achieved national visibility from the 1950s to the 1980s with major exhibitions in Dallas, Austin, Atlanta, Los Angeles, Detroit, and New York. A second book, Black Art in Houston: The Texas Southern University Experience, *appeared in 1978 to confirm the importance of his work and that of his faculty and students. Biggers died on January 25, 2001, in Houston.*

Source: Frank H. Wardlaw, "John Biggers: Artist," in Black Leaders, ed. by Barr and Calvert, pp. 191–220; Texas Highways 48, no. 12 (Dec., 2001): 40.

La Valle Wesley (left) *with grandmother Lora Lott Washington.* Institute of Texan Cultures illustration no. 95-320

Music provided African Americans in Texas with a form of entertainment that also served as a livelihood for the most talented. Drawing upon their nineteenth-century heritage of songs from fieldwork, weekend social gatherings, and religious spirituals, black musicians in the early twentieth century created the blues and ragtime. Scott Joplin became the best-known ragtime musician and composer from Texas. By the 1890s, he had moved from Texarkana to St. Louis and Sedalia, Missouri, where he worked as a piano player in saloons. There he met other African American musicians and began to publish first ballads and then marches that flowed into ragtime music, which demands foot tapping.

In 1899, Joplin wrote what Dave Oliphant calls "his most famous and influential composition, 'Maple Leaf Rag.'" Joplin continued to compose music including "Treemonisha," a ragtime folk opera in 1911. As Oliphant explains, "Many of the terms and techniques found in the titles and forms of Joplin's dance music would figure meaningfully in the later history of jazz." Major black musicians shaped in part by Joplin include "Fats" Waller, Louis Armstrong, and especially "Jelly Roll" Morton. Euday L. Bowman of Fort Worth added in 1914 the second most widely played ragtime composition, "Twelfth Street Rag," later recorded by Duke Ellington and Count Basie.[19]

Country blues joined ragtime as a major influence on the development of jazz. Texas country blues contained more humor and a lighter guitar style than other styles of blues. Henry "Ragtime Texas" Thomas probably began the style in the early twentieth century and recorded over twenty of his songs in the 1920s. "Cottonfield Blues" and "Texas Worried Blues" became the best known.

Blind Lemon Jefferson rose to great acclaim as the "King of the Country Blues." Jefferson took his Central Texas style by train to the larger towns of Dallas and Galveston in the World War I period. There he developed his unusual guitar style that included more improvising than most blues musicians. In the 1920s, he made over eighty recordings and became the most widely recognized male blues singer in the nation after moving to Chicago. His most popular songs include "Matchbox Blues" and "Long Lonesome Blues."

Although Jefferson influenced several blues singers, Huddie Ledbetter, nicknamed "Leadbelly," reflected the strongest connection to Jefferson in the country blues. Ledbetter made about 300 records, which "included almost every African American song form." Many found him "the most representative blues man of the Southwest"

Blind Lemon Jefferson. Institute of Texan Cultures illustration no. 70-848

according to Oliphant. "Irene" and "Ella Speed" ranked among his most famous songs.[20]

Classic blues appeared along with country blues in the early 1900s, but it came from the traveling minstrel show background. Several black female singers became popular with this style. Probably the best known, Beulah "Sippie" Wallace from Houston, appeared in the World War I period and began to record in Chicago and New York during the 1920s. Known as the "Texas Nightingale," she worked with Louis Armstrong and other jazz musicians to present her own songs such as "Special Delivery Blues" and "Trouble Everywhere I Roam," which reflected the influence of spirituals.[21]

Boogie-woogie came out of the lumber towns of East Texas to add a fourth style of music that helped shape jazz. The energetic

Huddie Ledbetter. Photograph by Bernice Abbott, 1946, courtesy of the Lead Belly Society

piano style and the "compositions of George W. Thomas and his brother Hersal" of Houston "were vital to the spread of this music." One of their compositions, "The Fives," reflected the strong influence of traveling musicians who played for workers laying the railroads across the state.[22]

From these diverse sources came jazz, with black musicians from Texas moving north to larger towns such as Kansas City where opportunities seemed greater. There in the 1920s the Bennie Moten band included an innovative trumpet soloist from Texarkana, Lammar Wright. Dallas developed its own popular entertainment district along Elm Street, called "Deep Ellum." Blind Lemon Jefferson had been joined there by Blind Willie Johnson who recorded what Alan Govenar and Jay Brakefield called the "holy blues," a musical style that included a strong influence from religion. Several blues piano players worked the area, including Alex Moore who continued into the 1960s.[23]

A variety of Texas musicians performed in Deep Ellum in the 1920s and 1930s, including the Blue Devils. The Oklahoma City band included saxophone player Buster Smith, trumpeter Oran "Hot Lips" Page, and trombonist and guitarist Eddie Durham. Several of the Texas musicians in the Blue Devils joined the Moten band in Kansas City during the 1930s. After Moten's death, a core of Texas musicians from his band joined what became the Count Basie orchestra that continued into the 1960s. The original Texans included Page Smith, Joe Keyes of Houston, Dan Minor, and Herschel Evans of Denton. In Kansas City during the late thirties and early forties, the Jay McShann orchestra featured new Texas jazzmen such as drummer Gus Johnson of Tyler and bass player Gene Ramey of Austin.[24]

Beginning in the 1920s, a stream of black and white jazz musicians left Texas to join New York, Chicago, and later Los Angeles bands and groups. Among the African Americans from Dallas, brothers Frederic "Keg" Johnson, a trombone player, and Budd Johnson, a saxophone player, joined Louis Armstrong's orchestra and later Cab Calloway and others in careers that continued from the 1930s to the 1970s.[25]

▼▼▼

Charlie Christian, an electric guitar player from Dallas who performed with Benny Goodman in the thirties and forties, helped shape the development of bebop. Out of Houston came Illinois Jacquet who joined Lionel Hampton and later Cab Calloway and Count Basie in the 1940s. Piano player Red Garland from Dallas moved to New York and became part of the Miles Davis Quintet in the fifties. Kenny Dorham from Central Texas attended Wiley College while developing as a trumpeter. He played with Dizzy Gillespie and Billy Eckstine in the forties and continued through the sixties. Out of Fort Worth in the 1940s came Ornette Coleman, a tenor player who emerged as a leader of groups that performed a freer style of jazz with more improvising. He toured from New York to London into the 1980s.[26]

An older strain of African American music evolved from spirituals into gospels. In the 1920s, Arizona J. Dranes became the first Texas woman to sing gospel music commercially. She joined touring groups and made records for a Chicago studio.[27]

Influenced by jazz and gospel music, the rhythm and blues style appeared in the late 1940s. A Texas version developed with Aaron "T-Bone" Walker, who in the words of Alan Govenar "introduced the electric guitar as a lead instrument" replacing the saxophone. Walker went on to play in Chicago and influenced later generations including B. B. King and Stevie Ray Vaughan. Earlier Walker had played at Don Robey's Bronze Peacock Club in Houston. There Robey first presented Clarence "Gatemouth" Brown in the late forties and soon developed the Peacock Recording Company to distribute Brown's music. Both Robey and Brown went on to important careers in music and promotion.[28]

Etta Moten took her talented voice to Broadway, where she appeared as a lead in *Porgy and Bess* in the 1940s, followed by movie roles. Barbara Conrad lost a major part in a student opera at the University of Texas in the 1950s because of racial tensions in the desegregation era. Yet she went on to international success at the Metropolitan Opera in New York and in several European countries.[29]

▼▼▼

From spirituals to gospel music, African American churches such as Sandridge Baptist Church in Egypt, Texas, have produced many talented musicians, c. 1950. Institute of Texan Cultures illustration no. 82-226

Sports joined music as another major form of entertainment, in this case developing out of the expanding public school systems and town teams, even in the segregated first half of the twentieth century. As black high schools increased from nineteen in 1900 to 150 by 1925, athletic teams began to appear. The white University Interscholastic League had formed in 1913, to regulate all extracurricular activities, but the Prairie View Interscholastic League (PVIL) organized only in the late 1930s as the number of black high schools increased. The PVIL continued in that role for three decades, from the forties through the sixties, and developed a playoff system that was won by a variety of teams primarily across the eastern half of the state. The teams became a source of school and community pride for African Americans as well as another proving ground for individual self worth. As the best players in football, baseball, and basketball went on to college, sports scholarships also became a path to increased education.[30]

In baseball, many players in the early twentieth century continued to enjoy the game beyond school as part of semiprofessional teams representing their towns or in cities representing their neighborhood or the business that employed them. The best players moved up to professional teams that traveled or played in larger cities outside the state.

A fine pitcher from Texas, Andrew "Rube" Foster, organized the Negro National League in 1920, an organization that continued into

Etta Moten, a star of stage and screen in the 1930s.
Institute of Texan Cultures illustration no. 68-965

Andrew "Rube" Foster (1879–1930)

Andrew "Rube" Foster won acclaim as a baseball pitcher, manager, and organizer of the Negro National League for African American professional baseball players. He was born on September 17, 1879, to parents active in the African Methodist Church at Calvert, Texas. In the 1890s, he played baseball for the Waco Yellow Jackets, a team that traveled to play games for pay, usually against other black teams in the years of segregation.

His talent attracted the attention of teams in larger cities such as Chicago and Philadelphia where he played professionally and became a student of pitching to go with his powerful fastball. His nickname "Rube" came from an exhibition game victory over Rube Waddell, a star pitcher

Texan Jack Johnson became the world's heavyweight champion July 4, 1910, in Reno Nevada. Institute of Texan Cultures illustration no. 68-1077

"Rube" Foster with a baseball team in their traveling clothes. Institute of Texan Cultures illustration no. 68-987

the 1950s. Several outstanding players also came from the Lone Star state, including one of the best shortstops, Willie Wells, and a fine catcher, Raleigh "Biz" Mackey. The popularity of professional baseball in a period of segregation led to the founding of the all-black Texas-Oklahoma-Louisiana League in 1929. The league ended in 1931 as a result of the Great Depression.[31]

After Jackie Robinson integrated the previously white major leagues in 1947, African American players from Texas including Ernie Banks and Frank Robinson followed him as professional stars. The Texas minor league teams began to sign on black players in 1952.[32]

The best black football players usually went on from high school to the African American colleges in Texas, but a few began to play for major universities in the Midwest during the 1950s. Abner Haynes at North Texas State University became the first black star at a formerly white Texas university in the same period. In 1964, Warren McVea joined the University of Houston team. The following year Jerry LeVias at Southern Methodist University and John Westbrook at Baylor University became the first African Americans to play in the Southwest Conference, with every football team integrating by 1970. Many of the black football players from Texas moved on to professional football teams, including Heisman Trophy winners like running back Earl Campbell at the University of Texas in 1977, quarterback Andre Ware at the University of Houston in 1989 and running back Ricky Williams at the University of Texas in 1998.[33]

Black men and women also achieved prominence in basketball. Nolan Richardson in the early 1960s became the first African American to attend Texas Western University, later renamed the University of Texas at El Paso. In the 1990s, he coached a national championship team at the University of Arkansas. Hakeem Olajuwon followed an outstanding career at the University of Houston in the 1980s with professional championships for the Houston Rockets in the mid-1990s. After being the scoring leader for the national champion Texas Tech Lady Raiders in 1993, Sheryl Swoopes helped the Houston Comets win professional basketball championships in the late nineties.[34]

in the all-white major leagues.

By 1910, he became part owner and manager as well as a player in Chicago. After unsuccessful early efforts, he formed the Negro National League in 1920, the first ongoing black professional baseball league, and served as its early president. Perhaps exhausted from managing a team and directing the league, in 1926 he began to suffer from mental problems and died on December 9, 1930. The Baseball Hall of Fame elected him to membership in 1981, honoring him as the "father of Negro baseball."

Source: Peterson, *Only the Ball Was White,* pp. 103–15; Fink, "African American Baseball in Texas," pp. 44–71; Tyler and Barnett, eds., *New Handbook of Texas,* v. 2, p. 1132.

African American athletes from Texas attained popular and economic successes in individual as well as team sports during the late twentieth century after desegregation brought change in the 1960s. Boxer Curtis Cokes captured the world welterweight title during the 1960s, while George Foreman became heavyweight champion twice, during the 1970s and later in the 1990s. Track sprinter and long jumper Carl Lewis, who lived and trained in Houston, won several Olympic gold medals in the 1990s.[35]

By the 1960s African Americans in Texas were poised to enter all occupations and professions. With education, more and more black Texans could enter the middle class, and many achieved fame and fortune.

CHAPTER 5

Voting, Desegregation, and Economic Opportunity in the Late Twentieth Century

*A*FRICAN AMERICANS living in Texas cities, with their stronger economic base, moved to the front in the struggle for civil and political rights in the United States from the 1920s to the 1950s. Once the National Association for the Advancement of Colored People (NAACP) had been founded in 1909, it expanded to create a Houston chapter by 1912. By 1919, Texas towns supported thirty-one local chapters of the NAACP with seven thousand members. After a membership decline in the late 1920s and 1930s, black business leaders in Dallas and Houston helped create the Texas State Conference of NAACP branches that grew to 170. Efforts of organizers such as Lulu White of Houston and Juanita Craft of Dallas made the Texas conference one of the largest in the United States during the 1940s and 1950s.[1]

The treatment of African Americans in the legal system though, needed many changes, as indicated in a 1940 legal case regarding blacks serving on juries:

> In Harris County, where petitioner, a negro, was indicted and con-
> victed of rape, negroes constitute over 20% of the population, and
> almost 10% of the poll-tax payers; a minimum of from three to six
> thousand of them measure up to the qualifications prescribed by

Texas statutes for grand jury service. The court clerk, called as a state witness and testifying from court records covering the years 1931 through 1938, showed that only 5 of the 384 grand jurors who served during that period were negroes; that of 512 persons summoned for grand jury duty, only 18 were negroes; that of these 18, the names of 13 appeared as the last name on the 16 man jury list, the custom being to select the 12 man grand jury in the order that the names appeared on the list . . .

It is the petitioner's contention that his conviction was based on an indictment obtained in violation of the provision of the Fourteenth Amendment that "No state shall . . . deny to any person within its jurisdiction the equal protection of the laws." And the contention that equal protection was denied him rests on a charge that Negroes were in 1938 and long prior thereto intentionally and systematically excluded from grand jury service solely on account of their race and color. . . .[2]

With NAACP support, Lawrence Nixon, a black doctor in El Paso, brought suit in 1924 to overturn the state law that required a white primary by political parties, which prevented African Americans from voting. Nixon won rulings in 1927 and 1932 that the state by law could not require or allow a segregated primary. When Texas Democrats continued the white primary under local party rules, Richard R. Grovey, a Houston barber, unsuccessfully challenged the practice during the 1930s. Finally, in 1942, black dentist Lonnie Smith of Houston, the Bayou City, with the aid of Texas and national attorneys funded by the NAACP, brought a new case to oppose the white primary. The U.S. Supreme Court responded in 1944, by ruling the segregated party election unconstitutional. As a result, African American voter registration in Texas rose steadily and in percentage ranked first or second in the South by the 1950s. These Texas white primary cases established the legal basis for similar cases in other states.[3]

Following their success in ending the white primary, black leaders worked through the Progressive Voters League and similar groups to register voters and provide political information. Although the poll tax still discouraged low-income voters, African American registration increased to almost 39 percent of potential black voters by 1958. Most of the new voters supported the Democratic Party. The percentage of registered black voters climbed to 61 percent in 1966, second highest in the South, after federal courts ruled against the poll tax, sixty-two years after its passage.

One-person, one-vote court decisions forced congressional, legislative, and local government redistricting in the 1960s and 1970s. This opened the way for the election of African American candidates such as Barbara Jordan from Houston, who not only served in the Texas senate but went on to achieve national prominence in the U.S. Congress. Mickey Leland and other African Americans represented Houston and Dallas districts and black interests in Congress during the 1980s and 1990s. Wilhelmina Delco from Austin became a major advocate for education in the Texas legislature. The most visible political leaders in Texas became black mayors, such as Ron Kirk in Dallas and Lee Brown in Houston, who represented coalitions of minority and moderate white voters in the 1990s.

Black political officeholders in Texas increased rapidly from 29 in 1970 to 305 in 1990. Yet that number ranked behind other states with higher percentages of black population. The percentage of

Congresswoman Barbara Jordan of Texas and others commissioned the USS Miller, *a navy ship named for African American Texan Doris Miller.* Institute of Texan Cultures illustration no. 73-1031

African American officeholders in Texas also remained below the black population percentage in the state.[4]

Black urban economic development led to educational advances in Texas. Literacy for African Americans in Texas stood at 47.5 percent in 1890, higher than in eleven other southern states. It rose steadily to 86.6 percent in 1930, the second highest in the South. In Houston, literacy rose to 93 percent in 1930, higher than all southern cities except Washington, D.C., and St. Louis. By the 1930s, the number of black students in Texas schools stood first in the South while the number of high school graduates ranked second in 1940. The number of African American teachers in Texas ranked second in the nation, while black college faculty outnumbered those in any other state by 1930.

By the beginning of the 1930s, black schools in Texas received more money per pupil than in any other southern state. Black teachers in Texas also received higher average salaries than in other southern states. Yet these figures remained clearly below spending and salaries for white pupils and teachers. To overcome one barrier, black teachers lobbied with some success for equalization of salaries in the 1940s. Black teachers in Dallas received equal pay in 1943 as a result of their lawsuit, which set a precedent for equalization in Houston and other cities and towns.[5]

To eliminate discrimination in higher education, the Texas Council of Negro Organizations joined with the NAACP to seek integration of the University of Texas Law School. Heman Sweatt, a Houston postal worker and college graduate, won his case before the United States Supreme Court in 1950 because of unequal facilities:

> . . . petitioner filed an application for admission to the University of Texas Law School for the February, 1946, term. His application was rejected solely because he is a Negro. Petitioner thereupon brought this suit for mandamus against the appropriate school officials, respondents here, to compel his admission. At that time, there was no law school in Texas, which admitted Negroes.

▼▼▼

The State trial court continued the case for six months to allow the State to supply substantially equal facilities . . . while petitioner's appeal was pending, such a school was made available, but petitioner refused to register therein.

A hearing was held on the issue of the equality of the educational facilities at the newly established school as compared with the University of Texas Law School. . . . The law school for Negroes, which was to have opened in February, 1947, would have had no independent faculty or library. The teaching was to be carried on by four members of the University of Texas Law School faculty, who were to maintain their offices at the University of Texas while teaching at both institutions. Few of the 10,000 volumes ordered for the library had arrived, nor was there a full-time librarian. . . . The school lacked accreditation.[6]

Thus, the U.S. Supreme Court reversed the state court decision and required desegregation of the University of Texas Law School. Black Texans again had established an important precedent, one that foreshadowed the better-known Brown decision of 1954–55.[7]

Black parents and students, even with a court order, found themselves turned away at schools in Mansfield in 1956 by Texas Rangers under orders from Governor Alan Shivers. The state, local school districts in East Texas, and some federal judges moved slowly on desegregation, as in Houston where even in 1961 only a few black students gained entrance into previously white schools. Foot dragging occurred despite the firm and reasonable efforts of the first African American school board member in Houston, Hattie Mae White, who had been a teacher.

The process of school desegregation continued through the 1960s and 1970s as new court cases led federal judges to require busing and other changes in some districts. In response many whites moved into the suburbs of large cities. Suits by African Americans also resulted in the election of school board members from single-member districts, which led to more minority representation. By the 1980s,

Heman Marion Sweatt was admitted to the University of Texas law school in 1950. Institute of Texan Cultures illustration no. 68-969

attention turned again to the courts in efforts to equalize funding for poor school districts that often included more minority students. High school graduates increased to 51.6 percent of African Americans in Texas over fifteen years old by 1980—slightly above the national average, but below the white level of 62 percent in Texas.

▼▼▼

Desegregation also occurred in Texas colleges and universities, although the percentage of African American students remained lower than the population percentage. The costs of higher education prohibited poorer black students from attending. Black faculty and administrators began to appear in previously white colleges in the 1970s and 1980s. Among the historically black colleges, Bishop closed because of financial problems, while others faced similar concerns. Texas Southern University, however, created during the 1940s by the state in a futile attempt to maintain segregation, grew into the largest of the black colleges in Texas with over eight thousand students by the 1980s. College graduates rose to 7 percent of African Americans in Texas over fifteen years of age by 1980, slightly above the national level but only half of the 15 percent for white Texans.[8]

In the Civil Rights movement of the 1950s and 1960s, Texas contributed an important leader to the Congress of Racial Equality. James Farmer, a graduate of Wiley College, helped lead the Freedom Rides of 1961 as well as later protests that attracted national attention. To desegregate public parks and transportation, black Texans continued court actions through the NAACP. In the 1960s, protest demonstrations began against segregated theaters and restaurants in towns and cities, usually by black college students with some support from white students. In Marshall, white-operated lunch counters closed to avoid desegregation after sit-ins by students from Bishop and Wiley colleges in 1960. Black and white students at the University of Texas and other colleges in Austin organized sit-ins and stand-ins at restaurants and theaters that same year. Through negotiations with moderate business leaders, desegregation began despite some continued opposition. In 1961, protests of segregated dormitories followed, although integration did not come until 1964.

Eldrewey Stearns helped form a student group at Texas Southern University that launched protests and sit-ins in Houston during 1960. The students found that white city and business leaders first tried to outlast them. After some debate, black students and community leaders agreed on a boycott of segregated stores that gained

The separate waiting room for African Americans at the Katy Railroad Depot. Institute of Texan Cultures illustration no. EN 19561.11

black middle-class support. Those efforts led white business leaders to agree upon unpublicized desegregation of lunch counters as a way of avoiding economic disruption. In 1961 protests of segregated theaters and economic discrimination met with growing success. Acting locally, often with only loose ties to national civil rights organization, Texas African American leaders began to crack the barriers of segregation in public places. During the national March on Washington in 1963, civil rights leaders in Texas conducted their own March in Austin to urge the implementation of the Civil Rights Act passed by Congress in 1964 to desegregate public places.[9]

With changes in the laws, some improvement was seen as more blacks found positions as law officers and judges. In Houston, the percentage of African Americans on the police force doubled in the 1960s and 1970s, and in the 1980s included the police chief, Lee Brown, who won the position of mayor in the 1990s.[10]

A United Klan meeting in Vidor, Texas, August 20, 1971. Institute of Texan Cultures illustration no. 90-64

Leon Coffee, Rodeo Bullfighting Clown

Leon Coffee of Blanco, Texas, a member of the Professional Rodeo Cowboy Association (PRCA), has been a bullfighter and rodeo clown since 1973. He started riding bulls when he was nine years old at a Little Britches Rodeo in Bastrop, Texas. He won the bareback riding, came in second in the bull riding, and won the best all-around cowboy.

When he started rodeoing they told him he would starve to death in the all-white rodeos of the times, so he painted his whole face white and put makeup on top of the white paint, wore white gloves, and topped it all with a pink wig.

Often the rodeo associations would not allow him to enter competitions, so he made the circuit of small rodeos in Texas. After he

Leon Coffee, rodeo bullfighter and clown from Blanco, Texas. Institute of Texan Cultures illustration no. 102-636

Economic opportunity for African Americans increased, as the average income rose from 37 percent of the white level in 1940 to 50 percent in 1960, and to about 60 percent by the 1970s. The War on Poverty federal programs during the administration of President Lyndon B. Johnson from Texas has done much to end racism as experienced for over 150 years by African Americans Texans.[11]

At the end of the twentieth century, discrimination still has not completely been obliterated. Laws have affected change and white people's attitudes have undergone some transformation. With greater equality and economic advancement blacks have been assimilated into the mainstream of society. While it is difficult to view as positive the segregation of blacks in the twentieth century it has had the unanticipated benefit of keeping alive a unique and distinct black culture in Texas. From the bonding together of blacks within their churches have come the displays of churchwomen in hats that today remain a source of glowing pride. The continuation of family reunions such as the descendants of Charley and Laura Willis, who formed their own family association and meet together in Texas to maintain the ties of the past, is another continuing tradition. From the "cast off" hog parts and the gathering of "greens" that provided bare sustenance for slaves has evolved the soul food coveted by many today. African American genealogy groups have formed in larger cities as individuals seek to reclaim their familial and cultural heritage. The Museum of African American Life and Culture has been developed in Dallas. Terry Cook, a graduate of Texas Tech University, began to perform with the Metropolitan Opera by the 1980s. By the 1990s, African American drama groups, such as the Ensemble Theater in Houston, formed in the larger cities. Holidays such as Juneteenth, Martin Luther King, Jr.'s birthday, and Kwanzaa now serve as opportunities for African Americans in Texas to come together to celebrate their unique contributions to the heritage of Texas. Out of adversity the black community has emerged with a vibrant culture that lives in Texas today.

raised a ruckus, they let him enter the bull riding event, and he won.

He started into bullfighting and clowning as a team with his friend Mike Moore, a Modoc Indian from Seguin, Texas. As clowns, it was their job to protect the cowboys who were trying to stay on the bulls for eight seconds. When cowboys got in trouble they did not much care what color the clowns were; they just wanted help!

Leon has worked every major rodeo in the United States and internationally. He has broken almost every bone in his body and had plastic surgery on his face. He continues to work the barrel at major rodeos, and his body is insured by an affiliate of Lloyd's of London.

Source: "Leon Coffee," Oral History Interview with Sara R. Massey, Institute of Texan Cultures, San Antonio (June 6, 2001).

Conclusion

*A*FRICAN AMERICANS from their first entry into Texas made cultural, economic, and social contributions to the region. In the colonial period of the sixteenth and seventeenth centuries free blacks and some slaves played roles in communities dominated by Texas Indians and by Spanish explorers and settlers. Additional free African Americans came from the United States to Mexican Texas in the early nineteenth century seeking greater opportunities for equal treatment and social mobility. Some fought in the Texas Revolution.

In the Republic and State of Texas slavery grew rapidly as a source of labor until the Civil War. Extreme limitations existed on the lives of slaves. The separation of families, restrictions on travel, and treatment as property made their lives harsh and difficult. Politicians made laws to control their work and everyday life. Despite handicaps, enslaved people showed skill and ingenuity by helping each other. African Americans found solace and joy in their communities and religion as they expressed themselves through storytelling, music, and folklore. When opportunities arose, they tried to escape to freedom into Mexico, and some succeeded.

In spite of continued discrimination after emancipation at the end of the Civil War, African Americans gained greater control over their lives, including marriages in their churches. They created new opportunities for education including colleges, voting rights, and finding diverse jobs with better wages. They established some small black towns and large neighborhoods in growing Texas cities.

In the twentieth century, some African Americans moved out of Texas to northern cities, while others looked for new jobs in Texas urban areas. Those jobs included work with railroads, oil companies, steel producers, ship builders, and as dockworkers. A black middle class opened businesses in the cities, where African American doctors, lawyers, writers, photographers, musicians, and sports figures found employment. By the mid-twentieth century, a growing black middle class led the way, even nationally at times, toward breaking down the barriers of discrimination, especially in court cases for voting rights, serving on juries, and ending segregation.

The lives of African Americans in Texas have not been easy. To gain equal treatment in society and to advance their social and economic status has taken the grit and passion of many. As Gloria Dean Randle Scott, a native of Houston says, "To get through you have to have a base. I see on whose shoulders we stand. Some of us only got through because they didn't."[1] The families, the churches, the businesses, the celebrations, the reunions, the stories, and the music have provided the bedrock for future generations of African Texans to grow and thrive as they make their continued contributions to the culture and society of the Lone Star State.

▼▼▼

Notes

CHAPTER 1. FREE AFRICAN AMERICANS BEFORE THE CIVIL WAR

1.   Rolena Adorno and Patrick Charles Pautz, *Álvar Núñez Cabeza de Vaca: His Account, His Life, and the Expedition of Pánfilo de Narváez,* vol. 1 (Lincoln: University of Nebraska Press, 1999), pp. 164–65, 414–22.

2.   Alwyn Barr, *Black Texans: The History of African Americans in Texas, 1528–1995,* 2d ed. (Norman: University of Oklahoma Press, 1996), pp. 2–3; Jack Jackson, *Los Mesteños: Spanish Ranching in Texas, 1721–1821* (College Station: Texas A&M University Press, 1986), p. 475.

3.   Barr, *Black Texans,* pp. 4–10.

CHAPTER 2. ENSLAVED AFRICAN AMERICANS BEFORE THE CIVIL WAR

1.   Barr, *Black Texans,* p. 17; B. A. Botkin, *Lay My Burden Down: A Folk History of Slavery* (Chicago: University of Chicago Press, 1945), p. 3.

2.   Randolph Campbell, *An Empire for Slavery: The Peculiar Institution in Texas, 1821–1865* (Baton Rouge: Louisiana State University Press, 1989) is the basis for this general account of slavery and slave roles in Texas.

3.   John Michael Vlach, *By the Work of Their Hands: Studies in Afro-American Folklife* (Charlottesville: University Press of Virginia, 1991), p. 86. Most of the quotations are from slave accounts that also may be seen in George P. Rawick, *The American Slave: A Composite Autobiography* (Westport, Conn.: Greenwood Press, 1972–79). Some also appear in Ron Tyler and Lawrence R. Murphy, eds., *The Slave Narratives of Texas* (Austin: Encino Press, 1974).

4.   Terry G. Jordan, *Texas Log Buildings: A Folk Architecture* (Austin: University of Texas Press, 1978), p. 15.

5.   Campbell, *Empire for Slavery,* pp. 122–23.

6.   Vlach, *By the Work of Their Hands,* p. 89.

7.   Ibid., p. 81.

8.   Ibid., pp. 85–86.

9.   Ibid., pp. 91–92; T. Lindsay Baker and Julie P. Baker, eds., *Till Freedom Cried Out: Memories of Texas Slave Life* (College Station: Texas A&M University Press, 1997), p. 107.

10. Vlach, *By the Work of Their Hands,* pp. 76–78; Baker and Baker, *Till Freedom Cried Out,* p. 113.

11. Vlach, *By the Work of Their Hands,* pp. 79–80; Karoline Patterson Bresenhan and Nancy O' Bryant Puentes, *Lone Stars: A Legacy of Texas Quilts, 1836–1936* (Austin: University of Texas Press, 1986), pp. 138–39.

12. Vlach, *By the Work of Their Hands,* pp. 90–91.

13. Ibid., pp. 94–95.

14. Campbell, *Empire for Slavery,* p. 159; Sara R. Massey, ed., *Black Cowboys of Texas* (College Station: Texas A&M University Press, 2000), pp. 39–47.

15. Campbell, *Empire for Slavery,* p. 166.

16. Ibid., pp. 201–203.

17. Ibid., pp. 169–74; quote on page 169.

18. Terry G. Jordan, *Texas Graveyards: A Cultural Legacy* (Austin: University of Texas Press, 1982), pp. 21–22, 47.

19. Campbell, *Empire for Slavery,* pp. 174–75.

20. Barr, *Black Texans,* p. 27.

21. Roger D. Abrahams, *Singing the Master: The Emergence of African-American Culture in the Plantation South* (New York: Pantheon Books, 1992); quotes from pp. xxiv, 310, 311, 314, 318.

22. Ruthe Winegarten, *Black Texas Women: A Sourcebook: Documents, Biographies, Timeline* (Austin: University of Texas Press, 1996), p. 35.

23. Campbell, *Empire for Slavery,* pp. 41, 179–85.

24. Ernest Wallace, David M. Vigness, and George B. Ward, eds., *Documents of Texas History,* 2d ed. (Austin: State House Press, 1994), p. 201.

25. Campbell, *Empire for Slavery,* pp. 247–50; quote on page 249.

CHAPTER 3. LIFE AFTER EMANCIPATION

1. Alwyn Barr, "Black Legislators of Reconstruction Texas," *Civil War History* 32 (Dec., 1986): 340–52; Merline Pitre, *Through Many Dangers, Toils and Snares: Black Leadership in Texas, 1868–1900* (Austin: Eakin Press, 1985).

2. Texas Historical Commission, *African Americans in Texas: Historical & Cultural Legacies* (Austin: Texas Historical Commission, 2000), pp. 17, 18, 31, 32; Ron Tyler and Douglas E. Barnett, eds., *The New Handbook of Texas,* vol. 2 (Austin: Texas State Historical Association, 1996), p. 221.

3. Alwyn Barr, "Black Migration into Southwestern Cities, 1865–1900," in *Essays on Southern History: Written in Honor of Barnes F. Lathrop,* edited by Gary W. Gallagher, 15–38 (Austin: The General Libraries, The University of Texas, 1980).

4. Texas Historical Commission, *African Americans in Texas,* pp. 13, 22, 27.

5. Barr, *Black Texans,* pp. 96–98.

6. Randolph Campbell, *Grass-Roots Reconstruction in Texas, 1865–1880* (Baton Rouge: Louisiana State University Press, 1997), p. 231.

7. Rebecca Sharpless, *Fertile Ground, Narrow Choices: Women on Texas Cotton Farms, 1900–1940* (Chapel Hill: University of North Carolina Press, 1999), pp. 122, 131, 163–66.

8. Massey, *Black Cowboys of Texas*, pp. 27, 44, 67–71, 247–52.

9. Ibid., pp. 108–11, 120, 143–46, 154–60.

10. Ibid., pp. 135–36, 193–203, 207–12.

11. Ibid., pp. 219–41.

12. Ibid., pp. 181–91.

13. Frank N. Schubert, *Black Valor: Buffalo Soldiers and the Medal of Honor, 1870–1898* (Wilmington, Del.: Scholarly Resources Inc., 1997), pp. 9–26.

14. Kevin Mulroy, *Freedom on the Border: The Seminole Maroons in Florida, the Indian Territory, Coahuila, and Texas* (Lubbock: Texas Tech University Press, 1993), pp. 117, 122–25; Schubert, *Black Valor*, pp. 27–40.

15. Texas Historical Commission, *African Americans in Texas*, pp. 17, 37.

16. James Smallwood, *Time of Hope, Time of Despair: Black Texans during Reconstruction* (Port Washington, N.Y.: Kennikat Press, 1981), pp. 45–50; Ruthe Winegarten, *Black Texas Women: 150 Years of Trial and Triumph* (Austin: University of Texas Press, 1995), pp. 45–51.

17. Patricia Smith Prather and Jane Clements Monday, *From Slave to Statesman: The Legacy of Joshua Houston, Servant to Sam Houston* (Denton: University of North Texas Press, 1993), pp. 123–24.

18. Smallwood, *Time of Hope, Time of Despair*, pp. 112–17; Winegarten, *Black Texas Women*, pp. 42–53.

19. Sharpless, *Fertile Ground, Narrow Choices*, pp. 27–28, 32, 55–56.

20. Smallwood, *Time of Hope, Time of Despair*, pp. 113, 123.

21. Massey, *Black Cowboys of Texas*, pp. 246–71.

22. Clyde McQueen, *Black Churches in Texas: A Guide to Historic Congregations* (College Station: Texas A&M University Press, 2000); Texas Historical Commission, *African Americans in Texas*.

23. Winegarten, *Black Texas Women: A Sourcebook*, p. 47.

24. Jacob Fontaine III and Gene Burd, *Jacob Fontaine: From Slavery to the Greatness of the Pulpit, Press, Public Service* (Austin: Eakin Press, 1983); Texas Historical Commission, *African Americans in Texas*, p. 13.

25. J. Mason Brewer, *Dog Ghosts* and *The Word on the Brazos* (Austin: University of Texas Press, 1976): *Dog Ghosts*, p. 3; *Word on the Brazos*, pp. 64–66; quote on page 11.

26. Smallwood, *Time of Hope, Time of Despair*, pp. 68–89.

27. Ibid., pp. 90–95.

28. Michael R. Heintze, *Private Black Colleges in Texas, 1865–1954* (College Station: Texas A&M University Press, 1985), p. 42.

29. Ibid., pp. 16–42.

30. George R. Woolfolk, *Prairie View: A Study in Public Conscience, 1878–1946* (New York: Pageant Press, 1962); Texas Historical Commission, *African Americans in Texas*.

31. Prather and Monday, *From Slave to Statesman*, pp. 77–238.

32. Dave Oliphant, *Texan Jazz* (Austin: University of Texas Press, 1996), pp. 12–15.

33. Massey, *Black Cowboys of Texas*, pp. 174–76.

CHAPTER 4. FROM DISCRIMINATION
TO PARTICIPATION DURING THE
TWENTIETH CENTURY

1. J. Morgan Kousser, *The Shaping of Southern Politics: Suffrage Restriction and the Establishment of the One-Party South, 1880–1910* (New Haven: Yale University Press, 1974), pp. 196–209; Alwyn Barr, *Reconstruction to Reform: Texas Politics, 1876–1906*, 2d ed. (Dallas: Southern Methodist University Press, 2000), pp. 193–208; Walter F. White, *Rope and Faggot: A Biography of Lynch* (New York: Knopf, 1929), pp. 21, 132–35, 158; Kenneth T. Jackson, *The Ku Klux Klan in the City, 1915–1930* (New York: Oxford University Press, 1967), p. 237; Barr, *Black Texans*, pp. 136–39.

2. Barr, *Black Texans*, pp. 140–42.

3. Gloria Dean Randle Scott in Brian Lanker, *I Dream a World: Portraits of Black Women Who Changed America* (New York: Stewart, Tabori, and Chang, 1989), p. 118.

4. Barr, *Black Texans*, pp. 147–56; Loren Schweninger, *Black Property Owners in the South, 1790–1915* (Urbana: University of Illinois Press, 1990), p. 81.

5. Ernest Obadele-Starks, *Black Unionism in the Industrial South* (College Station: Texas A&M University Press, 2000), pp. 3–36.

6. Ibid., pp. 37–52.

7. Ibid., pp. 53–67.

8. Ibid., pp. 68–81.

9. Ibid., pp. 82–100.

10. Barr, *Black Texans*, pp. 153–54.

11. Obadele-Starks, *Black Unionism*, pp. 101–11.

12. U.S. Bureau of the Census, *Negro Population, 1790–1915* (Washington, D.C.: Government Printing Office, 1918), pp. 91–93; U.S. Bureau of the Census, *Negroes in the United States, 1920–32* (Washington, D.C.: Government Printing Office, 1935), pp. 52–55; William J. Brophy, "The Black Texan, 1900–1950: A Quantitative History" (Ph.D. diss., Vanderbilt University, 1974), pp. 9–10, 25.

13. Brophy, "Black Texan," pp. 115, 117, 140; Walter C. Daniel, *Black Journals of the United States* (Westport: Greenwood Press, 1982), pp. 343–45; James Smallwood, "Texas," in *The Black Press in the South, 1865–1979*, edited by Henry Lewis Suggs (Westport: Greenwood Press, 1983), pp. 357–77; Barr, *Black Texans*, p. 153.

14. Bruce A. Glasrud, "Black Texans, 1900–1930" (Ph.D. diss., Texas Tech University, 1969), p. 127; Carter G. Woodson, *The Negro Professional Man and the Community* (New York: Negro Universities Press, 1969), p. 37; Schweninger, *Black*

Property Owners, p. 170; James M. SoRelle, "The Emergence of Black Business in Houston, Texas: A Study of Race and Ideology, 1919–1945" in *Black Dixie: Afro-Texan History and Culture in Houston,* edited by Howard Beeth and Cary D. Wintz (College Station: Texas A&M University Press, 1993), pp. 103–15.

15. Barr, *Black Texans,* p. 106.

16. Alwyn Barr, "African Americans in Texas: From Stereotypes to Diverse Roles," in *Texas through Time: Evolving Interpretations,* edited by Walter L. Buenger and Robert A. Calvert (College Station: Texas A&M University Press, 1991), p. 50; Winegarten, *Black Texas Women,* pp. 79–81, 194.

17. John Mason Brewer, ed., *Heralding Dawn: An Anthology of Verse* (Dallas: June Thomason, 1936); Barr, *Black Texans,* p. 171; Winegarten, *Black Texas Women,* pp. 144–45; Bernice Love Wiggins, *Tuneful Tales,* edited by Maceo C. Dailey and Ruthe Winegarten (1925; reprint, Lubbock: Texas Tech University Press, 2002).

18. Alan Govenar, *Portraits of Community: African American Photography in Texas* (Austin: Texas State Historical Association, 1996); Ruthe Winegarten and Sharon Kahn, *Brave Black Women: From Slavery to the Space Shuttle* (Austin: University of Texas Press, 1997), p. 74.

19. Oliphant, *Texan Jazz,* pp. 9–35.

20. Ibid., pp. 36–52; quote on page 51.

21. Ibid., pp. 53–73.

22. Ibid., pp. 74–82; quote on page 77.

23. Ibid., pp. 85–90; Alan B. Govenar and Jay F. Brakefield, *Deep Ellum and Central Track: Where the Black and White Worlds of Dallas Converged* (Denton: University of North Texas Press, 1998), pp. 61–134.

24. Oliphant, *Texan Jazz,* pp. 91–131.

25. Ibid., pp. 147–81.

26. Ibid., pp. 195–327.

27. Winegarten, *Black Texas Women,* p. 136.

28. Alan Govenar, *The Early Years of Rhythm and Blues: Focus on Houston* (Houston: Rice University Press, 1990), pp. 4–11.

29. Winegarten, *Black Texas Women,* pp. 138, 140.

30. Barr, *Black Texans,* pp. 100, 152; Ty Cashion, *Pigskin Pulpit: A Social History of Texas High School Football Coaches* (Austin: Texas State Historical Association, 1998), pp. 54, 117; *Dallas Morning News,* Dec. 23, 2001, pp. 2B, 23B.

31. Robert C. Fink, "African American Baseball in Texas, 1900–1950" (M.A. thesis, Texas Tech University, 1999).

32. Barr, *Black Texans,* p. 226.

33. Richard Pennington, *Breaking the Ice: The Racial Integration of Southwest Conference Football* (Jefferson, N.C.: McFarland & Company, 1987).

34. Barr, *Black Texans,* p. 246.

35. Ibid., pp. 246–47.

CHAPTER 5. VOTING, DESEGREGATION, AND ECONOMIC OPPORTUNITY IN THE LATE TWENTIETH CENTURY

1.   Charles Flint Kellogg, *NAACP: A History of the National Association for the Advancement of Colored People, 1909–1920,* vol. 1 (Baltimore: Johns Hopkins University Press, 1967), p. 239; Michael L. Gillette, "The Rise of the NAACP in Texas," *Southwestern Historical Quarterly* 81 (Apr., 1978): 393–416; Merline Pitre, *In Struggle against Jim Crow: Lulu B. White and the NAACP, 1900–1957* (College Station: Texas A&M University Press, 1999).

2.   Smith v. Texas: Negroes and Grand Jury Service, November 25, 1940 (331 U.S. 128–132, 85 L. ed. 84–87) in Wallace, Vigness, and Ward, *Documents of Texas History,* pp. 274–75.

3.   Darlene Clark Hine, *Black Victory: The Rise and Fall of the White Primary in Texas* (Millwood: KTO Press, 1979); Robert V. Haynes, "Black Houstonians and the White Democratic Primary, 1920–45," in *Black Dixie,* pp. 192–210.

4.   Joint Center for Political Studies, *National Roster of Black Elected Officials, July, 1975* (Washington, D.C., 1975), p. xxii; Joint Center for Political and Economic Studies, *Black Elected Officials: A National Roster 1990* (Washington, D.C., 1991), p. 10; Barr, *Black Texans,* pp. 176–79.

5.   Henry Allen Bullock, *A History of Negro Education in the South* (Cambridge: Harvard University Press, 1967), pp. 172, 180–81; U.S. Bureau of the Census, *Negroes in the United States, 1920–1932,* p. 237; James D. Anderson, *The Education of Blacks in the South, 1860–1936* (Chapel Hill: University of North Carolina Press, 1988), pp. 236–37; Woodson, *The Negro Professional Man,* p. 37.

6.   Sweatt v Painter: Desegregation of the University of Texas Law School, June 5, 1950 (339 U.S. 629–636, 94 L. ed. 1114–1120 [1950]) in Wallace, Vigness, and Ward, *Documents of Texas History,* pp. 280–81.

7.   Michael L. Gillette, "Blacks Challenge the White University," *Southwestern Historical Quarterly* 86 (Oct., 1982): 321–44.

8.   U.S. Bureau of the Census, *1980 Census of Population, Detailed Population Characteristics, Texas* (Washington, D.C.: Government Printing Office, 1983), pp. 59, 61; U.S. Bureau of the Census, *1980 Census of Population, Detailed Population Characteristics, U.S. Summary,* (Washington, D.C.: Government Printing Office, 1984), p. 45. See also Robyn Duff Ladino, *Desegregating Texas Schools: Eisenhower, Shivers, and the Crisis at Mansfield High* (Austin: University of Texas Press, 1996); William Henry Kellar, *Make Haste Slowly: Moderates, Conservatives, and School Desegregation in Houston* (College Station: Texas A&M University Press, 1999).

9.   Barr, *Black Texans,* pp. 184–87; Robert Goldberg, "Racial Change on the Southern Periphery: The Case of San Antonio, Texas, 1960–1965," *Journal of Southern History* 49 (Aug., 1983): 349–74; William Brophy, "Active Acceptance—Active Containment: The Dallas Story," in *Southern Businessmen and Desegregation,* edited by Elizabeth Jacoway and David R. Colburn (Baton Rouge: Louisiana State University

Press, 1982); Chandler Davidson, *Race and Class in Texas Politics* (Princeton: Princeton University Press, 1990), p. 249; Thomas R. Cole, *No Color Is My Kind: The Life of Eldrewey Stearns and the Integration of Houston* (Austin: University of Texas Press, 1997); Gail K. Beil, "Four Marshallites' Roles in the Passage of the Civil Rights Act of 1964," *Southwestern Historical Quarterly* 106 (July, 2002): 1–14; Martin Kuhlman, "Direct Action at the University of Texas during the Civil Rights Movement," *Southwestern Historical Quarterly* 98 (Apr., 1995): 551–56.

10.   Robert D. Bullard, *Invisible Houston: The Black Experience in Boom and Bust* (College Station: Texas A&M University Press, 1987), p. 107.

11.   U.S. Bureau of the Census, *1980 Census of Population, Detailed Population Characteristics, Texas, 1410, 1412;* U.S. Bureau of the Census, *1980 Census of Population, Detailed Population Characteristics, U.S. Summary,* pp. 551, 553; Bullard, *Invisible Houston,* pp. 32–75.

CONCLUSION

1.   Brian Lanker, *I Dream a World* (N.Y.: Stewart, Tabori, and Chang, 1989), p. 118.

Bibliographic Essay

For those who want to know more about various topics, the following comments are offered as a guide. Major sources used in writing this social and cultural account of African Americans in Texas are included.

The most up-to-date and elaborate listing of what has been written about black Texans is Bruce Glasrud and Laurie Champion, *Exploring the Afro-Texas Experience: A Bibliography of Secondary Sources About Black Texans* (Alpine, Tex.: Center for Big Bend Studies, Sul Ross State University, 2000).

Broad surveys include: Alwyn Barr, *Black Texans: A History of African Americans in Texas, 1528–1995,* 2d ed. (Norman: University of Oklahoma Press, 1996) and Ruthe Winegarten, *Black Texas Women: 150 Years of Trial and Triumph* (Austin: University of Texas Press, 1995). Another important general volume is Howard Beeth and Cary D. Wintz, eds., *Black Dixie: Afro-Texan History and Culture in Houston* (College Station: Texas A&M University Press, 1993).

For important black historical sites see Texas Historical Commission, *African Americans in Texas: Historical and Cultural Legacies* (Austin: Texas Historical Commission, 2000).

The longer biographical sketches in this account are based on articles in Ron Tyler and Douglas Barnett, eds., *The New Handbook of Texas* (Austin: Texas State Historical Association, 1996); and chapters on William M. McDonald by Bruce A. Glasrud, on Mary Branch by Olive D. Brown and Michael R. Heintze, and on John Biggers by Frank H. Wardlaw in Alwyn Barr and Robert A. Calvert, eds., *Black Leaders: Texans for Their Times* (Austin: Texas State Historical Association, 1981). For Maud Cuney Hare see Douglas Hales, *A Southern Family in Black and White: The Cuneys of Texas* (College Station: Texas A&M University Press, 2002). On "Rube" Foster consult Robert

Peterson, *Only the Ball Was White* (New York: Oxford University Press, 1970). Bessie Coleman is the subject of Doris L. Rich, *Queen Bess: Daredevil Aviator* (Washington, D.C.: Smithsonian Institution Press, 1993).

For important documents in African American history see Ruthe Winegarten, *Black Texas Women: A Sourcebook: Documents, Biographies, Timeline* (Austin: University of Texas Press, 1996) and Ernest Wallace, David M. Vigness, and George B. Ward, eds., *Documents of Texas History,* 2d ed. (Austin: State House Press, 1994).

On free African Americans before the Civil War, the best current volume is George R. Woolfolk, *The Free Negro in Texas, 1800–1860: A Study in Cultural Compromise* (Ann Arbor, Mich.: University Microfilms, 1976).

The basic study of slaves in Texas is Randolph B. Campbell, *An Empire for Slavery: The Peculiar Institution in Texas* (Baton Rouge: Louisiana State University Press, 1989).

The description of crafts by slave men and women is based primarily on John Michael Vlach, *By the Work of Their Hands: Studies in Afro-American Folklife* (Charlottesville: University Press of Virginia, 1991). Other information on slave culture and crafts may be found in Terry G. Jordan, *Texas Log Buildings: A Folk Architecture* (Austin: University of Texas Press, 1978); Terry G. Jordan, *Texas Graveyards: A Cultural Legacy* (Austin: University of Texas Press, 1982); and Roger D. Abrahams, *Singing the Master: The Emergence of African-American Culture in the Plantation South* (New York: Pantheon Books, 1992).

Useful selections of interviews with former slaves are in T. Lindsay Baker and Julie P. Baker, eds., *Till Freedom Cried Out: Memories of Texas Slave Life* (College Station: Texas A&M University Press, 1997) and Ron Tyler and Lawrence Murphy, eds., *The Slave Narratives of Texas* (Austin: Encino Press, 1974). A more elaborate collection of those accounts is in George W. Rawick, ed., *The American Slave: A Composite Autobiography* (Westport, Conn.: Greenwood Press, 1972–79), which includes several volumes of interviews conducted in Texas.

▼▼▼

The best general account of the post–Civil War period is James M. Smallwood, *Time of Hope, Time of Despair: Black Texans during Reconstruction* (Port Washington, N.Y.: Kennikat Press, 1981). See also Barry A. Crouch, *The Freedmen's Bureau and Black Texans* (Austin: University of Texas Press, 1992).

Several studies focus primarily on political and economic developments in the late nineteenth century. For black political leadership in that period the most detailed study is Merline Pitre, *Through Many Dangers, Toils, and Snares: Black Leadership in Texas, 1868–1900* (Austin: Eakin Press, 1985). See also Alwyn Barr, "Black Legislators of Reconstruction Texas," *Civil War History* 32 (Dec., 1986): 340–52 and Greg Cantrell, *Kenneth and John B. Rayner and the Limits of Southern Dissent* (Urbana and Chicago: University of Illinois Press, 1993).

The growth of urban population is discussed in Alwyn Barr, "Black Migration into Southwestern Cities, 1865–1900," in *Essays on Southern History: Written in Honor of Barnes F. Lathrop,* edited by Gary W. Gallagher, 15–38 (Austin: The General Libraries, The University of Texas, 1980). Insights into the postwar development of African American family life, property ownership, and education are found in Randolph B. Campbell, *Grass-Roots Reconstruction in Texas, 1865–1880* (Baton Rouge: Louisiana State University Press, 1997). Economic and social contributions of women in black families are considered by Rebecca Sharpless, *Fertile Ground, Narrow Choices: Women on Texas Cotton Farms, 1900–1940* (Chapel Hill: University of North Carolina Press, 1999).

The roles of African Americans in the cattle industry are discussed in Sara R. Massey, ed., *Black Cowboys of Texas* (College Station: Texas A&M University Press, 2000). Military service is the focus of Frank N. Schubert, *Black Valor: Buffalo Soldiers and the Medal of Honor, 1870–1898* (Wilmington, Del.: Scholarly Resources Inc., 1997) and Kevin Mulroy, *Freedom on the Border: The Seminole Maroons in Florida, the Indian Territory, Coahuila, and Texas* (Lubbock: Texas Tech University Press, 1993). See also Garna L. Christian, *Black Soldiers in Jim Crow Texas, 1899–1917* (College Station: Texas A&M University Press, 1995).

▼▼▼

A number of accounts explore various aspects of social life in the late nineteenth century. For religious developments the place to begin is Clyde McQueen, *Black Churches in Texas: A Guide to Historic Congregations* (College Station: Texas A&M University Press, 2000). The influence of one early minister is discussed in Jacob Fontaine III and Gene Burd, *Jacob Fontaine: From Slavery to the Greatness of the Pulpit, Press, Public Service* (Austin: Eakin Press, 1983). Folklore related to ministers is presented by J. Mason Brewer, *Dog Ghosts* and *The Word on the Brazos* (Austin: University of Texas Press, 1976). Commitment to the development of black education is reflected in Patricia Smith Prather and Jane Clements Monday, *From Slave to Statesman: The Legacy of Joshua Houston, Servant to Sam Houston* (Denton: University of North Texas Press, 1993). Colleges for African Americans are considered in George R. Woolfolk, *Prairie View: A Study in Public Conscience, 1878–1946* (New York: Pageant Press, 1962) and Michael R. Heintze, *Private Black Colleges in Texas, 1865–1954* (College Station: Texas A&M University Press, 1985).

Several volumes recount the limitations, including violence, faced by African Americans in political as well as economic and social activities. For voting problems see J. Morgan Kousser, *The Shaping of Southern Politics: Suffrage Restriction and the Establishment of the One-Party South, 1880–1910* (New Haven: Yale University Press, 1974) and Alwyn Barr, *Reconstruction to Reform: Texas Politics, 1876–1906*, 2d ed. (Dallas: Southern Methodist University Press, 2000). On violence see Walter White, *Rope and Faggot: A Biography of Judge Lynch* (New York: Knopf, 1929) and Kenneth T. Jackson, *The Ku Klux Klan in the City, 1915–1930* (New York: Oxford University Press, 1967).

Economic problems and advances for African Americans in the early twentieth century are described in Loren Schweninger, *Black Property Owners in the South, 1790–1915* (Urbana: University of Illinois Press, 1990) and Ernest Obadele-Starks, *Black Unionism in the Industrial South* (College Station: Texas A&M University Press, 2000).

Migration into Texas cities and the development of black businesses are considered in U.S. Bureau of the Census, *Negro Population, 1790–1915* (Washington, D.C.: Government Printing Office,

1918); U.S. Bureau of the Census, *Negroes in the United States, 1920–32* (Washington, D.C.: Government Printing Office, 1935); William J. Brophy, "The Black Texan, 1900–1950: A Quantitative History" (Ph.D. diss., Vanderbilt University, 1974); James Smallwood, "Texas," in *The Black Press in the South, 1865–1979,* edited by Henry Lewis Suggs (Westport: Greenwood Press, 1983); and James M. SoRelle, "The Emergence of Black Business in Houston, Texas: A Study of Race and Ideology, 1919–1945," in *Black Dixie,* edited by Beeth and Wintz, 103–15. The growth of a black middle class including professional people is explored by Carter G. Woodson, *The Negro Professional Man and the Community* (New York: Negro Universities Press, 1969) and Bruce A. Glasrud, "Black Texans, 1900–1930" (Ph.D. diss., Texas Tech University, 1969).

Cultural activities receive attention in several volumes, including black writers discussed in Ruthe Winegarten, *Black Texas Women;* Alwyn Barr, "African Americans in Texas: From Stereotypes to Diverse Roles," in *Texas through Time: Evolving Interpretations,* edited by Walter L. Buenger and Robert A. Calvert (College Station: Texas A&M University Press, 1991); and Bernice Love Wiggins, *Tuneful Tales,* edited by Maceo C. Dailey and Ruthe Winegarten (1925; reprint, Lubbock: Texas Tech University Press, 2002).

The contributions of another professional group are the focus of Alan Govenar, *Portraits of Community: African American Photography in Texas* (Austin: Texas State Historical Association, 1996). New musicians and their styles are discussed in Dave Oliphant, *Texan Jazz* (Austin: University of Texas Press, 1996); Alan B. Govenar and Jay F. Brakefield, *Deep Ellum and Central Track: Where the Black and White Worlds of Dallas Converged* (Denton: University of North Texas Press, 1998); and Alan Govenar, *The Early Years of Rhythm and Blues: Focus on Houston* (Houston: Rice University Press, 1990).

Black sports activities receive attention in Ty Cashion, *Pigskin Pulpit: A Social History of Texas High School Football Coaches* (Austin: Texas State Historical Association, 1998) and Robert C. Fink, "African American Baseball in Texas, 1900–1950" (M.A. thesis, Texas Tech University, 1999). The mid–twentieth century change to broader

▼▼▼

participation is described by Richard Pennington, *Breaking the Ice: The Racial Integration of Southwest Conference Football* (Jefferson, N.C.: McFarland & Company, 1987).

African American civil rights groups and their efforts are explored in Charles Flint Kellogg, *NAACP: A History of the National Association for the Advancement of Colored People, 1909–1920*, vol. 1 (Baltimore: Johns Hopkins University Press, 1967); Michael L. Gillette, "The Rise of the NAACP in Texas," *Southwestern Historical Quarterly* 81 (Apr., 1978): 393–416; and Merline Pitre, *In Struggle against Jim Crow: Lulu B. White and the NAACP, 1900–1957* (College Station: Texas A&M University Press, 1999).

The court cases to regain voting rights are the focus of Darlene Clark Hine, *Black Victory: The Rise and Fall of the White Primary in Texas* (Millwood: KTO Press, 1979) and Robert V. Haynes, "Black Houstonians and the White Democratic Primary, 1920–45," in *Black Dixie,* edited by Beeth and Wintz, 192–210. The growing number of African American political leaders becomes clear from a comparison of Joint Center for Political Studies, *National Roster of Black Elected Officials, July, 1975* (Washington, D.C., 1975) with Joint Center for Political and Economic Studies, *Black Elected Officials: A National Roster 1990* (Washington, D.C., 1991). See also Chandler Davidson, *Race and Class in Texas Politics* (Princeton: Princeton University Press, 1990).

Efforts to improve black schools are described in Henry Allen Bullock, *A History of Negro Education in the South* (Cambridge: Harvard University Press, 1967) and James D. Anderson, *The Education of Blacks in the South, 1860–1935* (Chapel Hill: University of North Carolina Press, 1988). Varied aspects of school desegregation are considered by Michael L. Gillette, "Blacks Challenge the White University," *Southwestern Historical Quarterly* 86 (Oct., 1982), 321–44; Robyn Duff Ladino, *Desegregating Texas Schools: Eisenhower, Shivers, and the Crisis at Mansfield High* (Austin: University of Texas Press, 1996); and William Henry Kellar, *Make Haste Slowly: Moderates, Conservatives, and School Desegregation in Houston* (College Station: Texas A&M University Press, 1999).

▼▼▼

The civil rights movement in Texas is presented in Robert Goldberg, "Racial Change on the Southern Periphery: The Case of San Antonio, Texas, 1960–1965," *Journal of Southern History* 49 (Aug., 1983): 349–74; William Brophy, "Active Acceptance—Active Containment: The Dallas Story," in *Southern Businessmen and Desegregation*, edited by Elizabeth Jacoway and David R. Colburn (Baton Rouge: Louisiana State University Press, 1982); and Thomas R. Cole, *No Color is My Kind: The Life of Eldrewey Stearns and the Integration of Houston* (Austin: University of Texas Press, 1997). Also see Gail K. Beil, "Four Marshallites' Roles in the Passage of the Civil Rights Act of 1964," *Southwestern Historical Quarterly* 106 (July, 2002): 1–14, and Martin Kuhlman, "Direct Action at the University of Texas during the Civil Rights Movement," *Southwestern Historical Quarterly* 98 (April, 1995):551–56.

The complexity of life for African Americans in a Texas city after the civil rights movement is explored in Robert D. Bullard, *Invisible Houston: The Black Experience in Boom and Bust* (College Station: Texas A&M University Press, 1987).

Index

▼▼▼

▼▼▼

race riots, 70

ragtime music, 76–77

railroads, 35, 38, 40, 45, 67–68, *68,* 80, 100

Ramey, Gene, 80

Ramirez, Pedro, 7

ranching: and cowboys, 37–40, *37, 39, 41,* 48, 62; by free African Americans before Civil War, 7, 8, 12; by slaves, 16

Ransom, Ethel, 64

Red River War (1874), 43

redistricting, 89

Redwine, W. A., 73

religion: of free African Americans before Civil War, 5, 7, 8, 12; in late nineteenth century, 38, 49–51, *51;* and ministers, 24, 35, 41, 49–51, 72, 73; music in churches, 80, *82;* of slaves, 23–24, 99. *See also specific churches*

Rendezvous with America (Tolson), 72

Republican Party, 34, *46,* 54, 63

rhythm and blues, 81

Rice, C. W., 67

Richardson, Clifton, Sr., 66–67

Richardson, James, 8

Richardson, Nolan, 85

Rio Grande, 28, 41

Robert (slave), 23

Roberts, Peyton, 35

Robey, Don, 81

Robinson, Frank, 85

Robinson, Harriet, 25–26

Robinson, Jackie, 85

Robison, Jack, 16–17, *17*

rodeo clown, 96–98, *96*

rodeos, 38–39, 96–98, *96*

Rogers, Will, 39

Roman Catholic Church, 5, 7, 8, 24, 50

Roquemore, Eugene, 75

runaway slaves, 23, 25, 27–28, 42, 99

Rusk County, 18, 25

Sabine River, 8

salaries of teachers, 90

sale of slaves, 14, *14,* 16, 21–23

Sam Houston Industrial and Training School, 59

Samuel Huston College, 57, 58, *60*

San Antonio: churches in, 49, *51;* domestic workers in, *45;* free African Americans in, before Civil War, 7, 12; Juneteenth in, *30;* population of blacks in, 35; Riegler Confectionary in, *71;* schools and college in, *34, 54,* 58; slaves in, 16–17; in Texas Revolution, 8

San Antonio River, 28

Sanderson, 38

San Jacinto, battle of, 8, *10*

school boards, 91

schools. *See* colleges, black; education

Schulenberg, *19*

Scott, Gloria Dean Randle, 100

seamstresses, 12, 17, 36–37

segregation: of Army, 40–41; Boyd's opposition to, 50; in late-nineteenth and twentieth centuries, 65–66, 93–96, *94;* of rodeos, 39, 96–97; of schools, 54–55; of sports, 84; and white primary, 63, 67, 88. *See also* prejudice and discrimination

Seguin, 57, 97

Seminole Indians, 42–43, 48

Seminole Negro Indian Scouts, 41–43, *44,* 48, 49

Sepia, 72

7D ranch, 38

Seven Stars of Consolidation of America, 32

sharecroppers, 36, 47, 66

shipbuilding, 70, 100

Shivers, Alan, 91

shoe making, 18

shouts, 59

Sidle, Carl, 75

Sigler, Henry, 12

Simpson (slave carpenter), 18

singers. *See* music

sit-ins, 93

slave laws, 16, 24

slave revolts, 27

slave trade, 13–14, *14*

slaves: from Africa, 13, *20,* 24; agricultural work by, 13, 15, 16; burial practices of, 24; children as, 14, 15–16, 21–23, 27; during Civil War, 28, *29;* clothing of, 15–21; crafts and skills of, 15, 16, 18–21, *19,* 24; culture of, 12, 24–27, 99; and education, 16, 24; Emancipation Proclamation for, 28, 30;

DATE DUE

GAYLORD			PRINTED IN U.S.A.

ISBN 1-58544-350-6

90000